The West of Owen Wister

Other Books by Robert L. Hough

*The Quiet Rebel: William Dean Howells
as Social Commentator* (1959)

Edited:

Satanstoe by James Fenimore Cooper (1962)

Literary Criticism of Edgar Allan Poe (1965)

The Rise of Silas Lapham by William Dean Howells
(1971)

THE WEST OF OWEN WISTER, 1860-1938

Selected Short Stories

Introduction by Robert L. Hough

A BISON BOOK

University of Nebraska Press · Lincoln

First Bison Book printing: April 1972

Most recent printing shown by first digit below:
2   3   4   5   6   7   8   9   10

Manufactured in the United States of America

Contents

Introduction

TODAY Owen Wister is remembered almost solely as the author of *The Virginian*. This novel, perhaps the most popular western ever written, has gone through countless editions, been presented in stage, television, and movie versions, and made its way generally into American folklore. The tall, lean, quiet cowboy with his sense of honor and fair play, love of the out-of-doors, and competence in his craft has become an American legend. He was and is the American adventurer, the American hero, and Wister is rightly remembered as the creator of many of his qualities and the writer of the first great novel about him.

Unfortunately, this fact has obscured others about Wister, the most important of which is that for a period of ten years at the turn of the century he was the first and most significant western local-color writer in American literature. His short stories, which embodied this tradition, have been forgotten, yet it was these stories that gave us our first real knowledge of the West's "wide, wild farm and ranch community, spotted with remote towns, and veined with infrequent railroads." And this West was not only that of the cowboy, but of the soldier, the seeker, the Indian, the hunter, even the priest. Moreover, Wister's depiction was given with an authenticity not hitherto found in American letters. In fact, the impulse to write of the West came from his desire to describe the region exactly as he had experienced it in the late 1880s and 1890s. He felt that no one before him had even attempted to depict the West:

> [One] Autumn evening of 1891, fresh from Wyoming and its wild glories, I sat in the club dining with a man as enamored of the West as I was. . . . From oysters to coffee we compared experiences. Why wasn't some Kipling saving the sagebrush for American literature, before the sagebrush and all that it signified went the way of the California forty-niner, the Mississippi steam-boat, went the way of everything? . . . What was fiction doing, fiction the only thing that has always outlived fact? Must it be perpetual teacups? Was Alkali Ike in the comic papers the one figure which the jejune American imagination, always at full-cock to banter or to brag, could discern in that epic which was being lived at a gallop out in the sagebrush? "To hell with tea-cups and the great American laugh," we two said, as we sat dining at the club. . . . "Walter, I'm going to try it myself!" I exclaimed . . . "I'm going to start this minute."[1]

And so he did, finishing most of "Hank's Woman," his first western story accepted for publication, that evening in the library of the Philadelphia Club.

The place of composition for this first story is significant. For Wister, like Bret Harte, with whom he

1. Owen Wister, *Roosevelt, The Story of a Friendship* (New York: Macmillan, 1930), p. 29.

was often compared, wrote of the West as an outsider, an observer who brought to his perceptions of the West all the advantages and disadvantages of an upper-class Philadelphia background. This "outside" point of view is clearly seen in many of the stories, where the central narrator is an eastern traveler or sportsman who observes and eventually is educated to western customs and ideas. Wister remained an easterner throughout his life, yet the West always exercised a tremendous fascination upon him. For the young man who had graduated summa cum laude from Harvard in 1882, studied music in Paris, and was preparing for a law career in Philadelphia, the first glimpse of the West in 1885 was a revelation. The rugged beauty, the freedom, the possibilities of the vast rolling plains and mountains stirred him deeply. "I don't wonder a man never comes back [east] after he has once been here a few years,"[2] he wrote in his Wyoming journal of 1885.

This fascination remained. In all, he was to make fifteen journeys to the West between 1885 and 1914, journeys which covered every Western state and often lasted over six months of the year. Even before his first story was accepted, Wister began to collect Western idioms, descriptions, anecdotes, and details of life that he was eventually to use in his stories. Beginning his career in the 1890s, he came near the end of a well-established tradition in American letters, that of the local-color story, and even though the region he dealt with had been virtually ignored as a legitimate area for

2. *Owen Wister Out West: His Journals and Letters,* ed. Fanny Kemble Wister (Chicago: University of Chicago Press, 1958), p. 30.

such stories, the influence of the tradition was strong. In Wister, as in many local-color writers, there is a definite attempt to capture the "feeling" or ambience of a region in the descriptions, the language, the customs and values. It is in this preoccupation with accuracy that Wister leaves Bret Harte and his predecessors in the dime westerns. One false touch destroyed a story for him and he went to great lengths to insure his knowledge. He was an outsider and knew it; so he took part in roundups and night herding, stayed for months at army posts, visited and revisited places where his stories took place. To correct errors he was continually reading his stories to western friends before publication and rewriting mistakes or false impressions. He tore up one piece because a Wells Fargo agent told him the holdup scene was wrong:

> I value accuracy more than any other quality in such stories as I write. I don't care how effective they are, if they're false, they're spoiled for me. I noticed a good instance of this in John Heard's story in the current *Cosmopolitan*, made from two real incidents of the army in Arizona both familiar to me previously. Heard makes his captain . . . use the sign language to the Indians. These southern Indians do not have the sign language.[3]

Yet despite such feelings for realism his main interest was essentially narrative and not local-color detail. He was a storyteller, not a purveyor of local tradition, and though he knew the roundup, night herding, and army camp life, details of these activities seldom figure significantly in the stories; they remain in the back-

3. Ibid., p. 223.

ground. For him, "the story was the thing," and like his friend Kipling with his tales of India, Wister seems to have seen himself as a preserver of the *stories* of the West. To be faithful to the locale, the language, the customs was important, but what Wister really sought was the tale or the incident. When he talked to soldiers, cowboys, or Indians, he wanted their stories, their adventures, their anecdotes.

> Captain Ray told some entertaining stories of a bibulous paymaster. He traveled with a secretary named Charley and a "jimmy-john" [Americanism for demijohn: a large whiskey container]. On one journey the stagecoach was overset on a mountain, a man's leg broken, and the stage demolished. The major was supposed to be dead among the ruins, but he poked his head out and cried to this distant-flung secretary, "Oh, Charley, is the jimmy-john hurt?" At Fort Robinson he had a German as orderly, who was supposed to attend to the officer's business when the officer was drunk. One day the Colonel and some visitors from New York arrived at the paymaster's quarters and found both master and man hopelessly intoxicated. Later the reckoning was overheard: "You dammed scoundrel, didn't I tell you you were not to get drunk unless I was sober?" "Yes, sir, but ven vas I going to haf my chance?"
> The Captain . . . promised to give me experiences for narration the next time I should call.[4]

Near the end of his career Wister wrote a brief summary of his writing philosophy: "Absorb, digest, perpend your subject; then try to interest your reader at

4. Ibid., pp. 177–78.

the start, and sweat to keep him interested to the finish."

For the modern reader this interest is not only in Wister's general merit as a storyteller or in his technical abilities, but often in a certain tension or ambivalence toward the West. From the first Wister found himself caught between romantic and realistic views. He was of course a well-to-do easterner looking at, filtering, perhaps even formulating the western experience. He could and did praise the physical beauty of the West and the kind of man he saw emerging in its environment: self-reliant, loyal, manly. The Virginian is the prototype, but there are others—Scipio Le Moyne, Specimen Jones, Lin McLean. These men are heroes on horseback, the Anglo-Saxon adventurers come to the American West, and Wister obviously viewed them with delight and pride.

Yet he saw the other side of the coin too. The land was often hostile and barren, physically and culturally—"the other side of the moon," he once called it— and those who came could be brutal or mean or weak. In 1891 he wrote:

> I begin to conclude, after five seasons of observation that life in this negligent, irresponsible wilderness tends to turn people shiftless, incompetent, and cruel. I noticed in Wolcott in 1885 and I notice today a sloth, in doing anything and everything, that is born of the deceitful ease with which makeshifts answer here.[5]

Characters and situations embodying these qualities appear in the stories, and it is interesting to note that

5. Ibid., p. 112.

as Wister grew older (and as the cowboys, forts, and open ranges disappeared), he became more skeptical of the advantages of the West. The stories published in *When West Was West* (1928) are more cynical and less in the heroic tradition than those in *Red Men and White* (1896), and *Lin McLean* (1898). The men of good conscience, the Chalkeyes and the Steptoe McDees, are still present, but the Pete Browns and the ruthless Salamancas become far more prominent. The focus is less on self-reliant men and how they win than on tricksters and how they win or are foiled. Interestingly, more of the later stories are set in the arid Southwest than in the valleys and mountains of Wyoming.

In any final assessment of Wister as a writer, one can certainly point to weaknesses. In the seventy to eighty short stories he wrote about the West, he was often over obvious, over sentimental, at times trite. The characterization is sometimes sketchy, almost caricature, and the stories too slight to bear the weight they should. But there is genuine merit too. Wister was often a fine storyteller with a real sense of plot and anecdote. He was an observant man who wrote what he saw and never corrupted his vision of the West into a sentimental stereotype, something he easily could have done after his early success. In his depiction of violence ("you're not going to get much American Western adventure without blood"), his description of language (which was often toned down for publication), and his account of local detail, Wister gave us a picture which we can accept. And he gave us the stories, the tales, the happenings as he came to know them.

Moreover, his stories include some suggestion of the variety of the "irrepressible country" and, though more muted, what he himself found so satisfying there: the sense of freedom and peace and beauty. In the final entry of his 1891 journal, written as he concluded his fifth summer in the West, Wister noted:

> September 11. I am pausing among the mountains [and] hunting alone, which I prefer. . . . Today is very beautiful, and I like to dwell on every detail of what surrounds me. My horse feeds by a swampy cold little stream, where the soft ground shows the recent tread of elk. A steady gentle wind is making the pines sing. The other sounds I hear being the furious scolding of a squirrel in a pine up the hill just behind me and the coarse call of the various mountain jays who fly across this opening in the woods, inspect me, and pass on; while here I bask in the comfortable sun, a willow bush for my head, my feet in some sagebrush, and look down and up the little green draws that come down through the pines to meet just here and make a brook which flows into Gros Ventre below. Could I "say to the passing moment stay!" I'd surely say it now.[6]

The selections in this volume represent a personal choice. Though they give some idea of the geographical range of Wister's settings and of his breadth in subject matter, they were chosen because they typify his considerable achievement in the short story. In them he seemed best able to combine his interest in factual

6. Ibid., p. 130.

detail, effective characterization, and dramatic narrative, elements he considered vital to any successful fiction.

ROBERT L. HOUGH

University of Nebraska

Bibliographical Note

OWEN WISTER published five volumes of western stories: *Red Men and White* (New York: Harper & Bros., 1896); *Lin McLean* (New York: Harper & Bros., 1898); *The Jimmyjohn Boss and Other Stories* (New York: Harper & Bros., 1900); *Members of the Family* (New York: Macmillan, 1911); and *When West Was West* (New York: Macmillan, 1928). In addition, several chapters of *The Virginian* (New York: Macmillan, 1902) originally appeared as short stories.

The stories in this collection are arranged chronologically in order of original publication. Three— "Little Big Horn Medicine" (June 1894), "The Second Missouri Compromise" (March 1895), and "A Pilgrim on the Gila" (November 1895)—were first collected in *Red Men and White*. "Hank's Woman," which first appeared in August 1892, was extensively revised before it was collected in *The Jimmyjohn Boss*, which also included "Padre Ignazio" (April 1900) and "Napoleon Shave-Tail" (no previous magazine publication). The texts reproduced here are those of the 1902 edition of *Red Men and White* and the first edition of *The Jimmyjohn Boss*.

Most Wister scholarship has centered on *The Virginian*. For more general information on Wister's short stories, his attitudes toward the West, and critical reaction to both, those interested should see *Owen Wister*

Out West: His Journals and Letters, edited by Fanny Kemble Wister (Chicago: University of Chicago Press, 1958); M. C. Boatright, "The American Myth Rides the Range: Owen Wister's Man on Horseback," *Southwest Review* 36: 157–63; Don D. Walker, "Wister, Roosevelt, and James: A Note on the Western," *American Quarterly* 12: 358–66; and Marvin Lewis, "Owen Wister: Caste Imprints in Western Letters," *Arizona Quarterly* 10: 147–56.

Hank's Woman

I

MANY fish were still in the pool; and though luck seemed to have left me, still I stood at the end of the point, casting and casting my vain line, while the Virginian lay and watched. Noonday's extreme brightness had left the river and the plain in cooling shadow, but spread and glowed over the yet undimmed mountains. Westward, the Tetons lifted their peaks pale and keen as steel through the high, radiant air. Deep down between the blue gashes of their cañons the sun sank long shafts of light, and the glazed laps of their snow-fields shone separate and white upon their lofty vastness, like handkerchiefs laid out to dry. Opposite, above the valley, rose that other range, the Continental Divide, not sharp, but long and ample. It was bare in some high places, and below these it stretched everywhere, high and low, in brown

3

and yellow parks, or in purple miles of pine a world of serene undulations, a great sweet country of silence.

A passing band of antelope stood herded suddenly together at sight of us; then a little breeze blew for a moment from us to them, and they drifted like phantoms away, and were lost in the levels of the sage-brush.

"If humans could do like that," said the Virginian, watching them go.

"Run, you mean?" said I.

"Tell a foe by the smell of him," explained the cow-puncher; "at fifty yards—or a mile."

"Yes," I said; "men would be hard to catch."

"A woman needs it most," he murmured. He lay down again in his lounging sprawl, with his grave eyes intently fixed upon my fly-casting.

The gradual day mounted up the hills farther from the floor of earth. Warm airs eddied in its wake slowly, stirring the scents of the plain together. I looked at the Southerner; and there was no guessing what his thoughts might be at work upon behind that drowsy glance. Then for a moment a trout rose, but only to look and whip down again into the pool that wedged its calm into the riffle from below.

"Second thoughts," mused the Virginian;

4

and as the trout came no more, "Second thoughts," he repeated; "and even a fish will have them sooner than folks has them in this mighty hasty country." And he rolled over into a new position of ease.

At whom or what was he aiming these shafts of truth? Or did he moralize merely because health and the weather had steeped him in that serenity which lifts us among the spheres? Well, sometimes he went on from these beginnings and told me wonderful things.

"I reckon," said he, presently, "that knowing when to change your mind would be pretty near knowledge enough for plain people."

Since my acquaintance with him—this was the second summer of it—I had come to understand him enough to know that he was unfathomable. Still, for a moment it crossed my thoughts that perhaps now he was discoursing about himself. He had allowed a jealous foreman to fall out with him at Sunk Creek ranch in the spring, during Judge Henry's absence. The man, having a brief authority, parted with him. The Southerner had chosen that this should be the means of ultimately getting the foreman dismissed and himself recalled. It was strategic. As he put it to me: "When I am gone, it will be right easy for the Judge to see which of us two he wants. And I'll not

5

have done any talking." All of which duly befell in the autumn as he had planned: the foreman was sent off, his assistant promoted, and the Virginian again hired. But this was meanwhile. He was indulging himself in a several months' drifting, and while thus drifting he had written to me. That is how we two came to be on our way from the railroad to hunt the elk and the mountain-sheep, and were pausing to fish where Buffalo Fork joins its waters with Snake River. In those days the antelope still ran there in hundreds, the Yellowstone Park was a new thing, and mankind lived very far away. Since meeting me with the horses in Idaho the Virginian had been silent, even for him. So now I stood casting my fly, and trusting that he was not troubled with second thoughts over his strategy.

"Have yu' studied much about marriage?" he now inquired. His serious eyes met mine as he lay stretched along the ground.

"Not much," I said; "not very much."

"Let's swim," he said. "They have changed their minds."

Forthwith we shook off our boots and dropped our few clothes, and heedless of what fish we might now drive away, we went into the cool, slow, deep breadth of backwater which the

6

bend makes just there. As he came up near me, shaking his head of black hair, the cow-puncher was smiling a little.

"Not that any number of baths," he remarked, "would conceal a man's objectionableness from an antelope—not even a she-one."

Then he went under water, and came up again a long way off.

We dried before the fire, without haste. To need no clothes is better than purple and fine linen. Then he tossed the flap-jacks, and I served the trout, and after this we lay on our backs upon a buffalo-hide to smoke and watch the Tetons grow more solemn, as the large stars opened out over the sky.

"I don't care if I never go home," said I.

The Virginian nodded. "It gives all the peace o' being asleep with all the pleasure o' feeling the widest kind of awake," said he. "Yu' might say the whole year's strength flows hearty in every waggle of your thumb." We lay still for a while. "How many things surprise yu' any more?" he next asked.

I began considering; but his silence had at length worked round to speech.

"Inventions, of course," said he, "these hyeh telephones an' truck yu' see so much about in the papers—but I ain't speaking o' such things of the brain. It is just the common things I

7

mean. The things that a livin', noticin' man is liable to see and maybe sample for himself. How many o' them kind can surprise yu' still?"

I still considered.

"Most everything surprised me onced," the cow-puncher continued, in his gentle Southern voice. "I must have been a mighty green boy. Till I was fourteen or fifteen I expect I was astonished by ten o'clock every morning. But a man begins to ketch on to folks and things after a while. I don't consideh that when—that afteh a man is, say twenty-five, it is creditable he should get astonished too easy. And so yu've not examined yourself that-a-way?"

I had not.

"Well, there's two things anyway—I know them for sure—that I expect will always get me—don't care if I live to thirty-five, or forty-five, or eighty. And one's the ways lightning can strike." He paused. Then he got up and kicked the fire, and stood by it, staring at me. "And the other is the people that other people will marry."

He stopped again; and I said nothing.

"The people that other people will marry," he repeated. "That will surprise me till I die."

"If my sympathy—" I began.

But the brief sound that he gave was answer enough, and more than enough cure for my levity.

"No," said he, reflectively; "not any such thing as a fam'ly for me, yet. Never, it may be. Not till I can't help it. And *that* woman has not come along so far. But I have been sorry for a woman lately. I keep thinking what she will do. For she will have to do something. Do yu' know Austrians? Are they quick in their feelings, like I-talians? Or are they apt to be sluggish, same as Norwegians and them other Dutch-speakin' races?"

I told him what little I knew about Austrians.

"This woman is the first I have ever saw of 'em," he continued. "Of course men will stampede into marriage in this hyeh Western country, where a woman is a scanty thing. It ain't what Hank has done that surprises me. And it is not on him that the sorrow will fall. For she is good. She is very good. Do yu' remember little black Hank? From Texas he claims he is. He was working on the main ditch over at Sunk Creek last summer when that Em'ly hen was around. Well, seh, yu' would not have pleasured in his company.

9

And this year Hank is placer-mining on Galena Creek, where we'll likely go for sheep. There's Honey Wiggin and a young fello' named Lin McLean, and some others along with the outfit. But Hank's woman will not look at any of them, though the McLean boy is a likely hand. I have seen that; for I have done a right smart o' business that-a-way myself, here and there. She will mend their clothes for them, and she will cook lunches for them any time o' day, and her conduct gave them hopes at the start. But I reckon Austrians have good religion."

"No better than Americans," said I.

But the Virginian shook his head. "Better'n what I've saw any Americans have. Of course I am not judging a whole nation by one citizen, and especially her a woman. And of course in them big Austrian towns the folks has shook their virtuous sayin's loose from their daily doin's, same as we have. I expect selling yourself brings the quickest returns to man or woman all the world over. But I am speakin' not of towns, but of the back country, where folks don't just merely arrive on the cyars, but come into the world the natural way, and grow up slow. Onced a week anyway they see the bunch of old grave-stones that marks their fam'ly. Their blood and name are knowed

10

about in the neighborhood, and it's not often
one of such will sell themselves. But their
religion ain't to them like this woman's. They
can be rip-snortin' or'n'ary in ways. Now she
is getting naught but hindrance and temptation and meanness from her husband and every
livin' thing around her—yet she keeps right
along, nor does she mostly bear any signs in
her face. She has cert'nly come from where
they are used to believing in God and a
hereafter mighty hard, and all day long. She
has got one o' them crucifixes, and Hank can't
make her quit prayin' to it. But what is she
going to do?"

"He will probably leave her," I said.

"Yes," said the Virginian — "leave her.
Alone; her money all spent; knowin' maybe
twenty words of English; and thousands of
miles away from everything she can understand. For our words and ways is all alike
strange to her."

"Then why did he want such a person?" I
exclaimed.

There was surprise in the grave glance which
the cow-puncher gave me. "Why, any man
would," he answered. "I wanted her myself,
till I found she was good."

I looked at this son of the wilderness, standing thoughtful and splendid by the fire, and

unconscious of his own religion that had unexpectedly shone forth in these last words. But I said nothing; for words too intimate, especially words of esteem, put him invariably to silence.

"I had forgot to mention her looks to yu'." he pursued, simply. "She is fit for a man." He stopped again.

"Then there was her wages that Hank saw paid to her," he resumed. "And so marriage was but a little thing to Hank—agaynst such a heap of advantages. As for her idea in takin' such as him—maybe it was that he was small and she was big; tall and big. Or maybe it was just his white teeth. Them ridiculous reasons will bring a woman to a man, haven't yu' noticed? But maybe it was just her sorrowful, helpless state, left stranded as she was, and him keeping himself near her and sober for a week.

"I had been seein' this hyeh Yellowstone Park, takin' in its geysers, and this and that, for my enjoyment; and when I found what they claimed about its strange sights to be pretty near so, I landed up at Galena Creek to watch the boys prospectin'. Honey Wiggin, yu' know, and McLean, and the rest. And so they got me to go down with Hank to Gardner for flour and sugar and truck, which we had to

wait for.   We lay around the Mammoth Springs
and Gardner for three days, playin' cyards with
friends.   And I got plumb inter-ested in them
tourists.   For I had partly forgot about Eastern people.   And hyeh they came fresh every
day to remind a man of the great size of his
country.   Most always they would talk to yu'
if yu' gave 'em the chance ; and I did.   I have
come mighty nigh regrettin' that I did not
keep a tally of the questions them folks asked
me.   And as they seemed genu-winely anxious
to believe anything at all, and the worser the
thing the believinger they'd grow, why I—
well, there's times when I have got to lie to
keep in good health.

"So I fooled and I fooled.   And one noon I
was on the front poach of the big hotel they
have opened at the Mammoth Springs for
tourists, and the hotel kid, bein' on the watch-
out, he sees the dust comin' up the hill, and he
yells out, 'Stage !'

"Yu've not saw that hotel yet, seh?   Well,
when the kid says 'Stage,' the consequences is
most sudden.   About as con-spicuous, yu' may
say, as when Old Faithful Geyser lets loose.
Yu' see, one batch o' tourists pulls out right
after breakfast for Norris Basin, leavin' things
empty and yawnin'.   By noon the whole hotel
outfit has been slumberin' in its chairs steady

13

for three hours. Maybe yu' might hear a fly buzz, but maybe not. Everything's liable to be restin', barrin' the kid. He's a-watchin' out. Then he sees the dust, and he says 'Stage!' and it touches the folks off like a hot pokeh. The Syndicate manager he lopes to a lookin'-glass, and then organizes himself behind the book; and the young photograph chap bounces out o' his private door like one o' them cuckoo-clocks; and the fossil man claws his specimens and curiosities into shape, and the porters line up same as parade, and away goes the piano and fiddles up-stairs. It is mighty con-spicuous. So Hank he come runnin' out from somewheres too, and the stage drives up.

"Then out gets a tall woman, and I noticed her yello' hair. She was kind o' dumb-eyed, yet fine to see. I reckon Hank noticed her too, right away. And right away her trouble begins. For she was a lady's maid, and her lady was out of the stage and roundin' her up quick. And it's 'Where have you put the keys, Willomene?' The lady was rich and stinkin' lookin', and had come from New Yawk in her husband's private cyar.

"Well, Willomene fussed around in her pockets, and them keys was not there. So she started explaining in tanglefoot English to her lady how her lady must have took them from her before leavin' the cyar. But the lady seemed to relish hustlin' herself into a rage. She got tolerable con-spicuous, too. And after a heap o' words, 'You are discharged,' she says; and off she struts. Soon her husband came out to Willomene, still standin' like statuary, and he pays her a good sum of cash, and he goes away, and she keeps a standing yet for a spell. Then all of a sudden she says something I reckon was 'O, Jesus,' and sits down and starts a cryin'.

"I would like to have given her comfort. But we all stood around on the hotel poach, and the right thing would not come into my haid. Then the baggage-wagon came in from Cinnabar, and they had picked the keys up on the road between Cinnabar and Gardner. So the lady and her toilet was rescued, but that did no good to Willomene. They stood her trunk down along with the rest—a brass-nailed little old concern—and there was Willomene out of a job and afoot a long, long ways from her own range; and so she kept sitting, and onced in a while she'd cry some more. We got her a room in the cheap hotel where the Park drivers sleeps when they're in at the Springs, and she acted grateful like, thanking the boys in her tanglefoot English. Next mawnin' her folks druv off in a private team to Norris

Basin, and she seemed dazed. For I talked with her then, and questioned her as to her wishes, but she could not say what she wished, nor if it was East or West she would go; and I reckon she was too stricken to have wishes.

"Our stuff for Galena Creek delayed on the railroad, and I got to know her, and then I quit givin' Hank cause for jealousy. I kept myself with the boys, and I played more cyards, while Hank he sca'cely played at all. One night I came on them—Hank and Willomene—walkin' among the pines where the road goes down the hill. Yu' should have saw that pair o' lovers. Her big shape was plain and kind o' steadfast in the moon, and alongside of her little black Hank! And there it was. Of course it ain't nothing to be surprised at that a mean and triflin' man tries to seem what he is not when he wants to please a good woman. But why does she get fooled, when it's so plain to other folks that are not givin' it any special thought? All the rest of the men and women at the Mammoth understood Hank. They knowed he was a worthless proposition. And I cert'nly relied on his gettin' back to his whiskey and openin' her eyes that way. But he did not. I met them next evening again by the Liberty Cap. Supposin' I'd been her brother or her mother, what

16

use was it me warning her? Brothers and mothers don't get believed.

"The railroad brought the stuff for Galena Creek, and Hank would not look at it on account of his courtin'. I took it alone myself by Yancey's and the second bridge and Miller Creek to the camp, nor I didn't tell Willomene good-bye, for I had got disgusted at her blindness."

The Virginian shifted his position, and jerked his overalls to a more comfortable fit. Then he continued:

"They was married the Tuesday after at Livingston, and Hank must have been pow'ful pleased at himself. For he gave Willomene a wedding present, with the balance of his cash, spending his last nickel on buying her a red-tailed parrot they had for sale at the First National Bank. The son-of-a-gun hollad so freely at the bank, the president nwde'd the cashier to get shed of the out-ragious bird, or he would wring its neck.

"So Hank and Willomene stayed a week up in Livingston on her money, and then he fetched her back to Gardner, and bought their grub, and bride and groom came up to the camp we had on Galena Creek.

"She had never slep' out before. She had never been on a hawss, neither. And she

17

mighty near rolled off down into Pitchstone Cañon, comin' up by the cut-off trail. Why, seh, I would not willingly take you through that place, except yu' promised me yu' would lead your hawss when I said to. But Hank takes the woman he had married, and he takes heavy-loaded pack-hawsses. 'Tis the first time such a thing has been known of in the country. Yu' remember them big tall grass-topped mountains over in the Hoodoo country, and how they descends slam down through the cross - timber that yu' can't sca'cely work through afoot, till they pitches over into lots an' lots o' little cañons, with maybe two inches of water runnin' in the bottom? All that is East Fork water, and over the divide is Clark's Fork, or Stinkin' Water, if yu' take the country yondeh to the southeast. But any place yu' go is them undesirable steep slopes, and the cut-off trail takes along about the worst in the business.

"Well, Hank he got his outfit over it somehow, and, gentlemen, hush! but yu'd ought t've seen him and that poor girl pull into our camp. Yu'd cert'nly never have conjectured them two was a weddin' journey. He was leadin', but skewed around in his saddle to jaw back at Willomene for riding so ignorant. Suppose it was a thing she was responsible for, yu'd not have talked to her that-a-way even in private ; and hyeh was the camp a-lookin', and a-listenin', and some of us ashamed. She was setting straddleways like a mountain, and between him and her went the three pack-animals, plumb shiverin' played out, and the flour—they had two hundred pounds—tilted over hellwards, with the red-tailed parrot shoutin' landslides in his cage tied on top o' the leanin' sacks.

"It was that mean to see, that shameless and unkind, that even a thoughtless kid like the McLean boy felt offended, and favorable to some sort of remonstrance. 'The son-of-a—!' he said to me. 'The son-of-a—! If he don't stop, let's stop him.' And I reckon we might have.

"But Hank he quit. 'Twas plain to see he'd got a genu-wine scare comin' through Pitchstone Cañon, and it turned him sour, so he'd hardly talk to us, but just mumbled 'How!' kind o' gruff, when the boys come up to congratulate him as to his marriage.

"But Willomene, she says when she saw me, 'Oh, I am so glad!' and we shook hands right friendly. And I wished I'd told her good-bye that day at the Mammoth. For she bore no spite, and maybe I had forgot her feelings in thinkin' of my own. I had talked to her down

19

at the Mammoth at first, yu' know, and she
said a word about old friends. Our friendship
was three weeks old that day, but I expect
her new experiences looked like years to her.
And she told me how near she come to gettin'
killed.

"Yu' ain't ever been over that trail, seh?
Yu' cert'nly must see Pitchstone Cañon. But
we'll not go there with packs. And we will
get off our hawsses a good ways back. For
many animals feels that there's something the
matter with that place, and they act very
strange about it.

" The Grand Cañon is grand, and makes yu'
feel good to look at it, and a geyser is grand
and all right, too. But this hyeh Pitchstone
hole, if Willomene had went down into that—
well, I'll tell yu', that you may judge.

" She seen the trail a-drawin' nearer and
nearer the aidge, between the timber and the
jumpin'-off place, and she seen how them little loose stones and the crumble stuff would
slide and slide away under the hawss's feet.
She could hear the stuff rattlin' continually
from his steps, and when she turned her haid
to look, she seen it goin' down close beside
her, but into what it went she could not see.
Only, there was a queer steam would come up
now and agayn, and her hawss trembled. So

she tried to get off and walk without sayin'
nothin' to Hank.   He kep' on ahaid, and her
hawss she had pulled up started to follo' as
she was half off him, and that gave her a tum-
ble, but there was an old crooked dead tree.   It
growed right out o' the aidge.   There she hung.

"Down below is a little green water tricklin', green as the stuff that gets on brass, and
tricklin' along over soft cream-colored formation, like pie.   And it ain't so far to fall but
what a man might not be too much hurt for
crawlin' out.   But there ain't no crawlin' out
o' Pitchstone Cañon, they say.   Down in there
is caves that yu' cannot see.   'Tis them that
coughs up the stream now and agayn.   With
the wind yu' can smell 'em a mile away, and
in the night I have been layin' quiet and heard
'em.   Not that it's a big noise, even when a
man is close up.   It's a fluffy kind of a sigh.   But
it sounds as if some awful thing was a-makin' it
deep down in the guts of the world.   They claim
there's poison air comes out o' the caves and
lays low along the water.   They claim if a bear
or an elk strays in from below, and the caves
sets up their coughin', which they don't regular every day, the animals die.   I have seen
it come in two seconds.   And when it comes
that-a-way risin' upon yu' with that fluffy kind
of a sigh, yu' feel mighty lonesome, seh.

21

"So Hank he happened to look back and see Willomene hangin' at the aidge o' them black rocks. And his scare made him mad. And his mad stayed with him till they come into camp. She looked around, and when she seen Hank's tent that him and her was to sleep in she showed surprise. And he showed surprise when he see the bread she cooked.

"'What kind of a Dutch woman are yu',' says he, strainin' for a joke, 'if yu' can't use a Dutch-oven?'

"'You say to me you have a house to live in,' says Willomene. 'Where is that house?'

"'I did not figure on gettin' a woman when I left camp,' says Hank, grinnin', but not pleasant, 'or I'd have hurried up with the shack I'm a buildin'.'

"He was buildin' one. When I left Galena Creek and come away from that country to meet you, the house was finished enough for the couple to move in. I hefted her brass-nailed trunk up the hill from their tent myself, and I watched her take out her crucifix. But she would not let me help her with that. She'd not let me touch it. She'd fixed it up agaynst the wall her own self her own way. But she accepted some flowers I picked, and set them in a can front of the crucifix. Then Hank he come in, and seein', says to me, 'Are you

22

one of the kind that squats before them silly dolls?' 'I would tell yu', I answered him; 'but it would not inter-est yu'.' And I cleared out, and left him and Willomene to begin their housekeepin'.

"Already they had quit havin' much to say to each other down in their tent. The only steady talkin' done in that house was done by the parrot. I've never saw any go ahaid of that bird. I have told yu' about Hank, and how when he'd come home and see her prayin' to that crucifix he'd always get riled up. He would mention it freely to the boys. Not that she neglected him, yu' know. She done her part, workin' mighty hard, for she was a willin' woman. But he could not make her quit her religion; and Willomene she had got to bein' very silent before I come away. She used to talk to me some at first, but she dropped it. I don't know why. I expect maybe it was hard for her to have us that close in camp, witnessin' her troubles every day, and she a foreigner. I reckon if she got any comfort, it would be when we was off prospectin' or huntin', and she could shut the cabin door and be alone."

The Virginian stopped for a moment.

"It will soon be a month since I left Galena Creek," he resumed. "But I cannot get the

business out o' my haid. I keep a studyin'
over it."

His talk was done. He had unburdened his
mind. Night lay deep and quiet around us,
with no sound far or near, save Buffalo Fork
plashing over its riffle.

II

We left Snake River. We went up Pacific
Creek, and through Two Ocean Pass, and down
among the watery willow-bottoms and beaver-
dams of the Upper Yellowstone. We fished;
we enjoyed existence along the lake. Then
we went over Pelican Creek trail and came
steeply down into the giant country of grass-
topped mountains. At dawn and dusk the elk
had begun to call across the stillness. And
one morning in the Hoodoo country, where we
were looking for sheep, we came round a jut of
the strange, organ-pipe formation upon a long-
legged boy of about nineteen, also hunting.

"Still hyeh?" said the Virginian, without
emotion.

"I guess so," returned the boy, equally mat-
ter-of-fact. "Yu' seem to be around yourself,"
he added.

They might have been next-door neighbors,

meeting in a town street for the second time in the same day.

The Virginian made me known to Mr. Lin McLean, who gave me a brief nod.

"Any luck?" he inquired, but not of me.

"Oh," drawled the Virginian, "luck enough."

Knowing the ways of the country, I said no word. It was bootless to interrupt their own methods of getting at what was really in both their minds.

The boy fixed his wide-open hazel eyes upon me. "Fine weather," he mentioned.

"Very fine," said I.

"I seen your horses a while ago," he said. "Camp far from here?" he asked the Virginian.

"Not specially. Stay and eat with us. We've got elk meat."

"That's what I'm after for camp," said McLean. "All of us is out on a hunt to-day—except him."

"How many are yu' now?"

"The whole six."

"Makin' money?"

"Oh, some days the gold washes out good in the pan, and others it's that fine it'll float off without settlin'."

"So Hank ain't huntin' to-day?"

"Huntin'! We left him layin' out in that

25

clump o' brush below their cabin. Been drinkin' all night."

The Virginian broke off a piece of the Hoo-doo mud-rock from the weird eroded pillar that we stood beside. He threw it into a bank of last year's snow. We all watched it as if it were important. Up through the mountain silence pierced the long quivering whistle of a bull-elk. It was like an unearthly singer practising an unearthly scale.

"First time she heard that," said McLean, "she was scared."

"Nothin' maybe to resemble it in Austria," said the Virginian.

"That's so," said McLean. "That's so, you bet! Nothin' just like Hank over there, neither."

"Well, flesh is mostly flesh in all lands, I reckon," said the Virginian. "I expect yu' can be drunk and disorderly in every language. But an Austrian Hank would be liable to respect her crucifix."

"That's so!"

"He 'ain't made her quit it yet?"

"Not him. But he's got meaner."

"Drunk this mawnin', yu' say?"

"That's his most harmless condition now."

"Nobody's in camp but them two? Her and him alone?"

"Oh, he dassent touch her."

"Who did he tell that to?"

"Oh, the camp is backin' her. The camp has explained that to him several times, you bet! And what's more, she has got the upper hand of him herself. She has him beat."

"How beat?"

"She has downed him with her eye. Just by endurin' him peacefully; and with her eye. I've saw it. Things changed some after yu' pulled out. We had a good crowd still, and it was pleasant, and not too lively nor yet too slow. And Willomene, she come more among us. She'd not stay shut in-doors, like she done at first. I'd have like to've showed her how to punish Hank."

"Afteh she had downed yu' with her eye?" inquired the Virginian.

Young McLean reddened, and threw a furtive look upon me, the stranger, the outsider. "Oh, well," he said, "I done nothing onusual. But that's all different now. All of us likes her and respects her, and makes allowances for her bein' Dutch. Yu' can't help but respect her. And she shows she knows."

"I reckon maybe she knows how to deal with Hank," said the Virginian.

"Shucks!" said McLean, scornfully. "And her so big and him so puny! She'd ought to lift him off the earth with one arm and lam him with a baste or two with the other, and he'd improve."

"Maybe that's why she don't," mused the Virginian, slowly; "because she is so big. Big in the spirit, I mean. She'd not stoop to his level. Don't yu' see she is kind o' way up above him and camp and everything—just her and her crucifix?"

"Her and her crucifix!" repeated young Lin McLean, staring at this interpretation, which was beyond his lively understanding. "Her and her crucifix. Turrible lonesome company! Well, them are things yu' don't know about. I kind o' laughed myself the first time I seen her at it. Hank, he says to me soft, 'Come here, Lin,' and I peeped in where she was a-prayin'. She seen us two, but she didn't quit. So I quit, and Hank came with me, sayin' tough words about it. Yes, them are things yu' sure don't know about. What's the matter with you camping with us boys to-night?"

We had been going to visit them the next day. We made it to-day, instead. And Mr. McLean helped us with our packs, and we carried our welcome in the shape of elk meat. So we turned our faces down the grass-topped mountains towards Galena Creek. Once, far through an open gap away below us, we sighted the cabin with the help of our field-glasses.

"Pity we can't make out Hank sleepin' in that brush," said McLean.

"He has probably gone into the cabin by now," said I.

"Not him! He prefers the brush all day when he's that drunk, you bet!"

"Afraid of her?"

"Well—oneasy in her presence. Not that she's liable to be in there now. She don't stay inside nowadays so much. She's been comin' round the ditch, silent-like but friendly. And she'll watch us workin' for a spell, and then she's apt to move off alone into the woods, singin' them Dutch songs of hern that ain't got no toon. I've met her walkin' that way, tall and earnest, lots of times. But she don't want your company, though she'll patch your overalls and give yu' lunch always. Nor she won't take pay."

Thus we proceeded down from the open summits into the close pines; and while we made our way among the cross-timber and over the little streams, McLean told us of various days and nights at the camp, and how Hank had come to venting his cowardice upon his wife's faith.

"Why, he informed her one day when he

was goin' to take his dust to town, that if he come back and found that thing in the house, he'd do it up for her. 'So yu' better pack off your wooden dummy somewheres,' says he. And she just looked at him kind o' stone-like and solemn. For she don't care for his words no more.

"And while he was away she'd have us all in to supper up at the shack, and look at us eatin' while she'd walk around puttin' grub on your plate. Day time she'd come around the ditch, watchin' for a while, and move off slow, singin' her Dutch songs. And when Hank comes back from spendin' his dust, he sees the crucifix same as always, and he says, 'Didn't I tell yu' to take that down?' 'You did,' says Willomene, lookin' at him very quiet. And he quit.

"And Honey Wiggin says to him, 'Hank, leave her alone.' And Hank, bein' all trembly from spreein' in town, he says, 'You're all agin me!' like as if he were a baby."

"I should think you would run him out of camp," said I.

"Well, we've studied over that some," McLean answered. "But what's to be done with Willomene?"

I did not know. None of us seemed to know.

"The boys got together night before last," continued McLean, "and after holdin' a unanimous meetin', we visited her and spoke to her about goin' back to her home. She was slow in corrallin' our idea on account of her bein' no English scholar. But when she did, after three of us takin' their turn at puttin' the proposition to her, she would not accept any of our dust. And though she started to thank us the handsomest she knowed how, it seemed to grieve her, for she cried. So we thought we'd better get out. She's tried to tell us the name of her home, but yu' can't pronounce such outlandishness."

As we went down the mountains, we talked of other things, but always came back to this; and we were turning it over still when the sun had departed from the narrow cleft that we were following, and shone only on the distant grassy tops which rose round us into an upper world of light.

"We'll all soon have to move out of this camp, anyway," said McLean, unstrapping his coat from his saddle and drawing it on. "It gets chill now in the afternoons. D'yu' see the quakin'-asps all turned yello', and the leaves keeps fallin' without no wind to blow 'em down? We're liable to get snowed in on short notice in this mountain country. If the

31

water goes to freeze on us we'll have to quit workin'. There's camp."

We had rounded a corner, and once more sighted the cabin. I suppose it may have been still half a mile away, upon the further side of a ravine into which our little valley opened. But field-glasses were not needed now to make out the cabin clearly, windows and door. Smoke rose from it; for supper-time was nearing, and we stopped to survey the scene. As we were looking, another hunter joined us, coming from the deep woods to the edge of the pines where we were standing. This was Honey Wiggin. He had killed a deer, and he surmised that all the boys would be back soon. Others had met luck besides himself; he had left one dressing an elk over the next ridge. Nobody seemed to have got in yet, from appearances. Didn't the camp look lonesome?

"There's somebody, though," said McLean.

The Virginian took the glasses. "I reckon —yes, that's Hank. The cold has woke him up, and he's comin' in out o' the brush."

Each of us took the glasses in turn; and I watched the figure go up the hill to the door of the cabin. It seemed to pause and diverge to the window. At the window it stood still, head bent, looking in. Then it returned quickly to the door. It was too far to discern, even through the glasses, what the figure was doing. Whether the door was locked, whether he was knocking or fumbling with a key, or whether he spoke through the door to the person within —I cannot tell what it was that came through the glasses straight to my nerves, so that I jumped at a sudden sound ; and it was only the distant shrill call of an elk. I was handing the glasses to the Virginian for him to see when the figure opened the door and disappeared in the dark interior. As I watched the square of darkness which the door's opening made, something seemed to happen there—or else it was a spark, a flash, in my own straining eyes.

But at that same instant the Virginian dashed forward upon his horse, leaving the glasses in my hand. And with the contagion of his act the rest of us followed him, leaving the pack animals to follow us as they should choose.

"Look!" cried McLean. "He's not shot her."

I saw the tall figure of a woman rush out of the door and pass quickly round the house.

"He's missed her!" cried McLean, again. "She's savin' herself."

But the man's figure did not appear in pursuit. Instead of this, the woman returned as quickly as she had gone, and entered the dark interior.

"She had something," said Wiggin. "What would that be?"

"Maybe it's all right, after all," said McLean. "She went out to get wood."

The rough steepness of our trail had brought us down to a walk, and as we continued to press forward at this pace as fast as we could, we compared a few notes. McLean did not think he saw any flash. Wiggin thought that he had heard a sound, but it was at the moment when the Virginian's horse had noisily started away.

Our trail had now taken us down where we could no longer look across and see the cabin. And the half-mile proved a long one over this ground. At length we reached and crossed the rocky ford, overtaking the Virginian there.

"These hawsses," said he, "are played out. We'll climb up to camp afoot. And just keep behind me for the present."

We obeyed our natural leader, and made ready for whatever we might be going into. We passed up the steep bank and came again in sight of the door. It was still wide open. We stood, and felt a sort of silence which the approach of two new-comers could not break. They joined us. They had been coming home from hunting, and had plainly heard a shot here. We stood for a moment more after learning this, and then one of the men called out the names of Hank and Willomene. Again we—or I at least—felt that same silence, which to my disturbed imagination seemed to be rising round us as mists rise from water.

"There's nobody in there," stated the Virginian. "Nobody that's alive," he added. And he crossed the cabin and walked into the door.

Though he made no gesture, I saw astonishment pass through his body, as he stopped still; and all of us came after him. There hung the crucifix, with a round hole through the middle of it. One of the men went to it and took it down; and behind it, sunk in the log, was the bullet. The cabin was but a single room, and every object that it contained could be seen at a glance; nor was there hiding-room for anything. On the floor lay the axe from the wood-pile; but I will not tell of its appearance. So he had shot her crucifix, her Rock of Ages, the thing which enabled her to bear her life, and that lifted her above life; and she—but there was the axe to show what she had done then. Was this cabin really empty? I looked more slowly about, half dreading to find that I had overlooked something. But it was as the Virginian had said; nobody was there.

As we were wondering, there was a noise

above our heads, and I was not the only one who started and stared. It was the parrot; and we stood away in a circle, looking up at his cage. Crouching flat on the floor of the cage, his wings huddled tight to his body, he was swinging his head from side to side; and when he saw that we watched him, he began a low croaking and monotonous utterance, which never changed, but remained rapid and continuous. I heard McLean whisper to the Virginian, "You bet he knows."

The Virginian stepped to the door, and then he bent to the gravel and beckoned us to come and see. Among the recent footprints at the threshold the man's boot-heel was plain, as well as the woman's broad tread. But while the man's steps led into the cabin, they did not lead away from it. We tracked his course just as we had seen it through the glasses: up the hill from the brush to the window, and then to the door. But he had never walked out again. Yet in the cabin he was not; we tore up the half-floor that it had. There was no use to dig in the earth. And all the while that we were at this search the parrot remained crouched in the bottom of his cage, his black eye fixed upon our movements.

"She has carried him," said the Virginian. "We must follow up Willomene."

The latest heavy set of footprints led us from the door along the ditch, where they sank deep in the softer soil; then they turned off sharply into the mountains.

"This is the cut-off trail," said McLean to me. "The same he brought her in by."

The tracks were very clear, and evidently had been made by a person moving slowly. Whatever theories our various minds were now shaping, no one spoke a word to his neighbor, but we went along with a hush over us.

After some walking, Wiggin suddenly stopped and pointed.

We had come to the edge of the timber, where a narrow black cañon began, and ahead of us the trail drew near a slanting ledge, where the footing was of small loose stones. I recognized the odor, the volcanic whiff, that so often prowls and meets one in the lonely woods of that region, but at first I failed to make out what had set us all running.

"Is he looking down into the hole himself?" some one asked; and then I did see a figure, the figure I had looked at through the glasses, leaning strangely over the edge of Pitchstone Cañon, as if indeed he was peering to watch what might be in the bottom.

We came near. But those eyes were sightless, and in the skull the story of the axe was carved. By a piece of his clothing he was hooked in the twisted roots of a dead tree, and hung there at the extreme verge. I went to look over, and Lin McLean caught me as I staggered at the sight I saw. He would have lost his own foothold in saving me had not one of the others held him from above.

She was there below; Hank's woman, brought from Austria to the New World. The vision of that brown bundle lying in the water will never leave me, I think. She had carried the body to this point; but had she intended this end? Or was some part of it an accident? Had she meant to take him with her? Had she meant to stay behind herself? No word came from these dead to answer us. But as we stood speaking there, a giant puff of breath rose up to us between the black walls.

"There's that fluffy sigh I told yu' about," said the Virginian.

"He's talkin' to her! I tell yu' he's talkin' to her!" burst out McLean, suddenly, in such a voice that we stared as he pointed at the man in the tree. "See him lean over! He's sayin', 'I have yu' beat after all.'" And McLean fell to whimpering.

Wiggin took the boy's arm kindly and walked him along the trail. He did not seem twenty yet. Life had not shown this side of itself to him so plainly before.

"Let's get out of here," said the Virginian.

It seemed one more pitiful straw that the lonely bundle should be left in such a vault of doom, with no last touches of care from its fellow-beings, and no heap of kind earth to hide it. But whether the place is deadly or not, man dares not venture into it. So they took Hank from the tree that night, and early next morning they buried him near camp on the top of a little mound.

But the thought of Willomene lying in Pitchstone Cañon had kept sleep from me through that whole night, nor did I wish to attend Hank's burial. I rose very early, while the sunshine had still a long way to come down to us from the mountain-tops, and I walked back along the cut-off trail. I was moved to look once more upon that frightful place. And as I came to the edge of the timber, there was the Virginian. He did not expect any one. He had set up the crucifix as near the dead tree as it could be firmly planted.

"It belongs to her, anyway," he explained.

Some lines of verse came into my memory, and with a change or two I wrote them as deep as I could with my pencil upon a small board that he smoothed for me.

"Call for the robin redbreast and the wren,
  Since o'er shady groves they hover,
  And with flowers and leaves do cover
The friendless bodies of unburied men.
  Call to this funeral dole
  The ant, the field-mouse, and the mole,
To rear her hillocks that shall keep her warm."

"That kind o' quaint language reminds me of a play I seen onced in Saynt Paul," said the Virginian. "About young Prince Henry."

I told him that another poet was the author.

"They are both good writers," said the Virginian. And as he was finishing the monument that we had made, young Lin McLean joined us. He was a little ashamed of the feelings that he had shown yesterday, a little anxious to cover those feelings with brass.

"Well," he said, taking an offish, man-of-the-world tone, "all this fuss just because a woman believed in God."

"You have put it down wrong," said the Virginian; "it's just because a man didn't."

Little Big Horn Medicine

SOMETHING new was happening among the Crow Indians. A young pretender had appeared in the tribe. What this might lead to was unknown alike to white man and to red; but the old Crow chiefs discussed it in their councils, and the soldiers at Fort Custer, and the civilians at the agency twelve miles up the river, and all the white settlers in the valley discussed it also. Lieutenants Stirling and Haines, of the First Cavalry, were speculating upon it as they rode one afternoon.

"Can't tell about Indians," said Stirling. "But I think the Crows are too reasonable to go on the warpath."

"Reasonable!" said Haines. He was young, and new to Indians.

"Just so. Until you come to his superstitions, the Indian can reason as straight as you or I. He's perfectly logical."

"Logical!" echoed Haines again. He held the regulation Eastern view that the Indian knows nothing but the three blind appetites.

"You'd know better," remarked Stirling, "if you'd been fighting 'em for fifteen years. They're as shrewd as Æsop's fables."

Just then two Indians appeared round a bluff —

one old and shabby, the other young and very gaudy —riding side by side.

"That's Cheschapah," said Stirling. "That's the agitator in all his feathers. His father, you see, dresses more conservatively."

The feathered dandy now did a singular thing. He galloped towards the two officers almost as if to bear them down, and, steering much too close, flashed by yelling, amid a clatter of gravel.

"Nice manners," commented Haines. "Seems to have a chip on his shoulder."

But Stirling looked thoughtful. "Yes," he muttered, "he has a chip."

Meanwhile the shabby father was approaching. His face was mild and sad, and he might be seventy. He made a gesture of greeting. "How!" he said, pleasantly, and ambled on his way.

"Now there you have an object-lesson," said Stirling. "Old Pounded Meat has no chip. The question is, are the fathers or the sons going to run the Crow Nation?"

"Why did the young chap have a dog on his saddle?" inquired Haines.

"I didn't notice it. For his supper, probably—probably he's getting up a dance. He is scheming to be a chief. Says he is a medicine-man, and can make water boil without fire; but the big men of the tribe take no stock in him—not yet. They've seen soda-water before. But I'm told this water-boiling astonishes the young."

"You say the old chiefs take no stock in him *yet*?"

"Ah, that's the puzzle. I told you just now Indians could reason."

"And I was amused."

"Because you're an Eastern man. I tell you, Haines, if it wasn't my business to shoot Indians I'd study them."

"You're a crank," said Haines.

But Stirling was not a crank. He knew that so far from being a mere animal, the Indian is of a subtlety more ancient than the Sphinx. In his primal brain —nearer nature than our own—the directness of a child mingles with the profoundest cunning. He believes easily in powers of light and darkness, yet is a sceptic all the while. Stirling knew this; but he could not know just when, if ever, the young charlatan Cheschapah would succeed in cheating the older chiefs; just when, if ever, he would strike the chord of their superstition. Till then they would reason that the white man was more comfortable as a friend than as a foe, that rations and gifts of clothes and farming implements were better than battles and prisons. Once their superstition was set alight, these three thousand Crows might suddenly follow Cheschapah to burn and kill and destroy.

"How does he manage his soda-water, do you suppose?" inquired Haines.

"That's mysterious. He has never been known to buy drugs, and he's careful where he does his trick. He's still a little afraid of his father. All Indians are. It's queer where he was going with that dog."

Hard galloping sounded behind them, and a courier from the Indian agency overtook and passed them, hurrying to Fort Custer. The officers hurried too, and, arriving, received news and orders. Forty Sioux were reported up the river coming to visit the Crows. It was peaceable, but untimely. The Sioux agent over at Pine Ridge had given these forty permission to go, without first finding out if it would be convenient to the Crow agent to have them come. It is a rule of the Indian Bureau that if one tribe desire to visit another, the agents of both must consent. Now, most of the Crows were farming and quiet, and it was not wise that a visit from the Sioux and a season of feasting should tempt their hearts and minds away from the tilling of the soil. The visitors must be taken charge of and sent home.

"Very awkward, though," said Stirling to Haines. He had been ordered to take two troops and arrest the unoffending visitors on their way. "The Sioux will be mad, and the Crows will be madder. What a bungle! and how like the way we manage Indian affairs!" And so they started.

Thirty miles away, by a stream towards which Stirling with his command was steadily marching through the night, the visitors were gathered. There was a cook-fire and a pot, and a stewing dog leaped in the froth. Old men in blankets and feathers sat near it, listening to young Cheschapah's talk in the flighty lustre of the flames. An old squaw acted as interpreter between Crow and Sioux. Round about, at a certain distance, the figures of the crowd lounged at the edge of the darkness. Two grizzled squaws stirred the pot, spreading a clawed fist to their eyes against the red heat of the coals, while young Cheschapah harangued the older chiefs.

"And more than that, I, Cheschapah, can do," said he, boasting in Indian fashion. "I know how to make the white man's heart soft so he cannot fight." He paused for effect, but his hearers seemed uninterested. "You have come pretty far to see us," resumed the orator, "and I, and my friend Two

46

Whistles, and my father, Pounded Meat, have come a day to meet you and bring you to our place. I have brought you a fat dog. I say it is good the Crow and the Sioux shall be friends. All the Crow chiefs are glad. Pretty Eagle is a big chief, and he will tell you what I tell you. But I am bigger than Pretty Eagle. I am a medicine-man."

He paused again; but the grim old chiefs were looking at the fire, and not at him. He got a friendly glance from his henchman, Two Whistles, but he heard his father give a grunt.

That enraged him. "I am a medicine-man," he repeated, defiantly. "I have been in the big hole in the mountains where the river goes, and spoken there with the old man who makes the thunder. I talked with him as one chief to another. I am going to kill all the white men."

At this old Pounded Meat looked at his son angrily, but the son was not afraid of his father just then. "I can make medicine to bring the rain," he continued. "I can make water boil when it is cold. With this I can strike the white man blind when he is so far that his eyes do not show his face."

He swept out from his blanket an old cavalry sabre painted scarlet. Young Two Whistles made a movement of awe, but Pounded Meat said, "My son's tongue has grown longer than his sword."

Laughter sounded among the old chiefs. Cheschapah turned his impudent yet somewhat visionary face upon his father. "What do you know of medicine?" said he. "Two sorts of Indians are among the Crows to-day," he continued to the chiefs. "One sort are the fathers, and the sons are the other. The young warriors are not afraid of the white man. The old

47

plant corn with the squaws. Is this the way with the Sioux?"

"With the Sioux," remarked a grim visitor, "no one fears the white man. But the young warriors do not talk much in council."

Pounded Meat put out his hand gently, as if in remonstrance. Other people must not chide his son.

"You say you can make water boil with no fire?" pursued the Sioux, who was named Young-man-afraid-of-his-horses, and had been young once.

Pounded Meat came between. "My son is a good man," said he. "These words of his are not made in the heart, but are head words you need not count. Cheschapah does not like peace. He has heard us sing our wars and the enemies we have killed, and he remembers that he has no deeds, being young. When he thinks of this sometimes he talks words without sense. But my son is a good man."

The father again extended his hand, which trembled a little. The Sioux had listened, looking at him with respect, and forgetful of Cheschapah, who now stood before them with a cup of cold water.

"You shall see," he said, "who it is that talks words without sense."

Two Whistles and the young bucks crowded to watch, but the old men sat where they were. As Cheschapah stood relishing his audience, Pounded Meat stepped up suddenly and upset the cup. He went to the stream and refilled it himself. "Now make it boil," said he.

Cheschapah smiled, and as he spread his hand quickly over the cup, the water foamed up.

"Huh!" said Two Whistles, startled.

The medicine-man quickly seized his moment.

48

"What does Pounded Meat know of my medicine?" said he. "The dog is cooked. Let the dance begin."

The drums set up their dull, blunt beating, and the crowd of young and less important bucks came from the outer circle nearer to the council. Cheschapah set the pot in the midst of the flat camp, to be the centre of the dance. None of the old chiefs said more to him, but sat apart with the empty cup, having words among themselves. The flame reared high into the dark, and showed the rock wall towering close, and at its feet the light lay red on the streaming water. The young Sioux stripped naked of their blankets, hanging them in a screen against the wind from the jaws of the cañon, with more constant shouts as the drumming beat louder, and strokes of echo fell from the black cliffs. The figures twinkled across each other in the glare, drifting and alert, till the dog-dance shaped itself into twelve dancers with a united sway of body and arms, one and another singing his song against the lifted sound of the drums. The twelve sank crouching in simulated hunt for an enemy back and forth over the same space, swinging together.

Presently they sprang with a shout upon their feet, for they had taken the enemy. Cheschapah, leading the line closer to the central pot, began a new figure, dancing the pursuit of the bear. This went faster; and after the bear was taken, followed the elk-hunt, and a new sway and crouch of the twelve gesturing bodies. The thudding drums were ceaseless; and as the dance went always faster and always nearer the dog pot, the steady blows of sound inflamed the dancers; their chests heaved, and their arms and bodies swung

49

alike as the excited crew filed and circled closer to the pot, following Cheschapah, and shouting uncontrollably. They came to firing pistols and slashing the air with knives, when suddenly Cheschapah caught up a piece of steaming dog from the pot, gave it to his best friend, and the dance was done. The dripping figures sat quietly, shining and smooth with sweat, eating their dog-flesh in the ardent light of the fire and the cool splendor of the moon. By-and-by they lay in their blankets to sleep at ease.

The elder chiefs had looked with distrust at Cheschapah as he led the dance; now that the entertainment was over, they rose with gravity to go to their beds.

"It is good for the Sioux and the Crows to be friends," said Pounded Meat to Young-man-afraid-of-his-horses. "But we want no war with the white man. It is a few young men who say that war is good now."

"We have not come for war," replied the Sioux. "We have come to eat much meat together, and remember that day when war was good on the Little Horn, and our warriors killed Yellow Hair and all his soldiers."

Pounded Meat came to where he and Cheschapah had their blankets.

"We shall have war," said the confident son to his father. "My medicine is good."

"Peace is also pretty good," said Pounded Meat. "Get new thoughts. My son, do you not care any more for my words?"

Cheschapah did not reply.

"I have lived a long while. Yet one man may be wrong. But all cannot be. The other chiefs say what I say. The white men are too strong."

"They would not be too strong if the old men were not cowards."

"Have done," said the father, sternly. "If you are a medicine-man, do not talk like a light fool."

The Indian has an "honor thy father" deep in his religion too, and Cheschapah was silent. But after he was asleep, Pounded Meat lay brooding. He felt himself dishonored, and his son to be an evil in the tribe. With these sore notions keeping him awake, he saw the night wane into gray, and then he heard the distant snort of a horse. He looked, and started from his blankets, for the soldiers had come, and he ran to wake the sleeping Indians. Frightened, and ignorant why they should be surrounded, the Sioux leaped to their feet; and Stirling, from where he sat on his horse, saw their rushing, frantic figures.

"Go quick, Kinney," he said to the interpreter, "and tell them it's peace, or they'll be firing on us."

Kinney rode forward alone, with one hand raised; and seeing that sign, they paused, and crept nearer, like crafty rabbits, while the sun rose and turned the place pink. And then came the parley, and the long explanation; and Stirling thanked his stars to see they were going to allow themselves to be peaceably arrested. Bullets you get used to; but after the firing's done, you must justify it to important personages who live comfortably in Eastern towns and have never seen an Indian in their lives, and are rancid with philanthropy and ignorance.

Stirling would sooner have faced Sioux than sentimentalists, and he was fervently grateful to these savages for coming with him quietly without obliging him to shoot them. Cheschapah was not behaving so amiably; and recognizing him, Stirling understood

51

about the dog. The medicine-man, with his faithful Two Whistles, was endeavoring to excite the prisoners as they were marched down the river to the Crow Agency.

Stirling sent for Kinney. " Send that rascal away," he said. " I'll not have him bothering here."

The interpreter obeyed, but with a singular smile to himself. When he had ordered Cheschapah away, he rode so as to overhear Stirling and Haines talking. When they speculated about the soda-water, Kinney smiled again. He was a quiet sort of man. The people in the valley admired his business head. He supplied grain and steers to Fort Custer, and used to say that business was always slow in time of peace.

By evening Stirling had brought his prisoners to the agency, and there was the lieutenant of Indian police of the Sioux come over from Pine Ridge to bring them home. There was restlessness in the air as night fell round the prisoners and their guard. It was Cheschapah's hour, and the young Crows listened while he declaimed against the white man for thwarting their hospitality. The strong chain of sentinels was kept busy preventing these hosts from breaking through to fraternize with their guests. Cheschapah did not care that the old Crow chiefs would not listen. When Pretty Eagle remarked laconically that peace was good, the agitator laughed ; he was gaining a faction, and the faction was feeling its oats. Accordingly, next morning, though the prisoners were meek on being started home by Stirling with twenty soldiers, and the majority of the Crows were meek at seeing them thus started, this was not all. Cheschapah, with a yelling swarm of his young friends, began to buzz about the column as it marched up the river. All had rifles.

"It's an interesting state of affairs," said Stirling to Haines. "There are at least fifty of these devils at our heels now, and more coming. We've got twenty men. Haines, your Indian experiences may begin quite early in your career."

"Yes, especially if our prisoners take to kicking."

"Well, to compensate for spoiling their dinner-party, the agent gave them some rations and his parting blessing. It may suffice."

The line of march had been taken up by ten men in advance, followed in the usual straggling fashion by the prisoners, and the rear-guard was composed of the other ten soldiers under Stirling and Haines. With them rode the chief of the Crow police and the lieutenant of the Sioux. This little band was, of course, far separated from the advance-guard, and it listened to the young Crow bucks yelling at its heels. They yelled in English. Every Indian knows at least two English words; they are pungent, and far from complimentary.

"It's got to stop here," said Stirling, as they came to a ford known as Reno's Crossing. "They've got to be kept on this side."

"Can it be done without gunpowder?" Haines asked.

"If a shot is fired now, my friend, it's war, and a court of inquiry in Washington for you and me, if we're not buried here. Sergeant, you will take five men and see the column is kept moving. The rest remain with me. The prisoners must be got across and away from their friends."

The fording began, and the two officers went over

to the east bank to see that the instructions were carried out.

"See that?" observed Stirling. As the last of the rear-guard stepped into the stream, the shore they were leaving filled instantly with the Crows. "Every man jack of them is armed. And here's an interesting development," he continued.

It was Cheschapah riding out into the water, and with him Two Whistles. The rear guard passed up the trail, and the little knot of men with the officers stood halted on the bank. There were nine—the two Indian police, the two lieutenants, and five long muscular boys of K troop of the First Cavalry. They remained on the bank, looking at the thick painted swarm that yelled across the ford.

"Bet you there's a hundred," remarked Haines.

"You forget I never gamble," murmured Stirling. Two of the five long boys overheard this, and grinned at each other, which Stirling noted; and he loved them. It was curious to mark the two shores : the feathered multitude and its yells and its fifty yards of rifles that fronted a small spot of white men sitting easily in the saddle, and the clear, pleasant water speeding between. Cheschapah and Two Whistles came tauntingly towards this spot, and the mass of Crows on the other side drew forward a little.

"You tell them," said Stirling to the chief of the Crow police, "that they must go back."

Cheschapah came nearer, by way of obedience.

"Take them over, then," the officer ordered.

The chief of Crow police rode to Cheschapah, speaking and pointing. His horse drew close, shoving the horse of the medicine-man, who now launched an insult that with Indians calls for blood. He struck

54

the man's horse with his whip, and at that a volume
of yells chorussed from the other bank.

"Looks like the court of inquiry," remarked Stirling. "Don't shoot, boys," he commanded aloud.

The amazed Sioux policeman gasped. "You not
shoot?" he said. "But he hit that man's horse—all
the same hit your horse, all the same hit you."

"Right. Quite right," growled Stirling. "All the
same hit Uncle Sam. But we soldier devils have orders to temporize." His eye rested hard and serious
on the party in the water as he went on speaking with
jocular unconcern. "Tem-po-rize, Johnny," said he.
"You savvy temporize?"

"Ump! Me no savvy."

"Bully for you, Johnny. Too many syllables. Well,
now! he's hit that horse again. One more for the
court of inquiry. Steady, men! There's Two Whistles switching now. They ought to call that lad
Young Dog Tray. And there's a chap in paint fool-
ing with his gun. If any more do that—it's very
catching— Yes, we're going to have a circus. Attention! Now what's that, do you suppose?"

An apparition, an old chief, came suddenly on the
other bank, pushing through the crowd, grizzled and
little and lean, among the smooth, full-limbed young
blood. They turned and saw him, and slunk from
the tones of his voice and the light in his ancient eye.
They swerved and melted among the cotton-woods,
so that the ford's edge grew bare of dusky bodies and
looked sandy and green again. Cheschapah saw the
wrinkled figure coming, and his face sank tame. He
stood uncertain in the stream, seeing his banded
companions gone and the few white soldiers firm on
the bank. The old chief rode to him through the

55

water, his face brightened with a last flare of command.

"Make your medicine!" he said. "Why are the white men not blind? Is the medicine bad to-day?" And he whipped his son's horse to the right, and to the left he slashed the horse of Two Whistles, and, whirling the leather quirt, drove them cowed before him and out of the stream, with never a look or word to the white men. He crossed the sandy margin, and as a man drives steers to the corral, striking spurs to his horse and following the frightened animals close when they would twist aside, so did old Pounded Meat herd his son down the valley.

"Useful old man," remarked Stirling; "and brings up his children carefully. Let's get these prisoners along."

"How rural the river looks now!" Haines said, as they left the deserted bank.

So the Sioux went home in peace, the lieutenants, with their command of twenty, returned to the post, and all white people felt much obliged to Pounded Meat for his act of timely parental discipline—all except one white person.

Sol Kinney sauntered into the agency store one evening. "I want ten pounds of sugar," said he, "and navy plug as usual. And say, I'll take another bottle of the Seltzer fizz salts. Since I quit whiskey," he explained, "my liver's poorly."

He returned with his purchase to his cabin, and set a lamp in the window. Presently the door opened noiselessly, and Cheschapah came in.

"Maybe you got that now?" he said, in English.

The interpreter fumbled among bottles of liniment and vaseline, and from among these household remedies brought the blue one he had just bought. Cheschapah watched him like a child, following his steps round the cabin. Kinney tore a half-page from an old Sunday *World*, and poured a little heap of salts into it. The Indian touched the heap timidly with his finger. "Maybe no good," he suggested.

"Heap good!" said the interpreter, throwing a pinch into a glass. When Cheschapah saw the water effervesce, he folded his newspaper with the salt into a tight lump, stuck the talisman into his clothes, and departed, leaving Mr. Kinney well content. He was doing his best to nourish the sinews of war, for business in the country was discouragingly slack.

Now the Crows were a tribe that had never warred with us, but only with other tribes; they had been valiant enough to steal our cattle, but sufficiently discreet to stop there; and Kinney realized that he had uphill work before him. His dearest hopes hung upon Cheschapah, in whom he thought he saw a development. From being a mere humbug, the young Indian seemed to be getting a belief in himself as something genuinely out of the common. His success in creating a party had greatly increased his conceit, and he walked with a strut, and his face was more unsettled and visionary than ever. One clear sign of his mental change was that he no longer respected his father at all, though the lonely old man looked at him often with what in one of our race would have been tenderness. Cheschapah had been secretly maturing a plot ever since his humiliation at the crossing, and now he was ready. With his lump of newspaper carefully treasured, he came to Two Whistles.

"Now we go," he said. "We shall fight with the Piegans. I will make big medicine, so that we shall get many of their horses and women. Then Pretty Eagle will be afraid to go against me in the council. Pounded Meat whipped my horse. Pounded Meat can cut his hay without Cheschapah, since he is so strong."

But little Two Whistles wavered. "I will stay here," he ventured to say to the prophet.

"Does Two Whistles think I cannot do what I say?"

"I think you make good medicine."

"You are afraid of the Piegans."

"No, I am not afraid. I have hay the white man will pay me for. If I go, he will not pay me. If I had a father, I would not leave him." He spoke pleadingly, and his prophet bore him down by ridicule. Two Whistles believed, but he did not want to lose the money the agent was to pay for his hay. And so, not so much because he believed as because he was afraid, he resigned his personal desires.

The next morning the whole band had disappeared with Cheschapah. The agent was taken aback at this marked challenge to his authority — of course they had gone without permission—and even the old Crow chiefs held a council.

Pretty Eagle resorted to sarcasm. "He has taken his friends to the old man who makes the thunder," he said. But others did not feel sarcastic, and one observed, "Cheschapah knows more than we know."

"Let him make rain, then," said Pretty Eagle. "Let him make the white man's heart soft."

The situation was assisted by a step of the careful Kinney. He took a private journey to Junction City, through which place he expected Cheschapah to return, and there he made arrangements to have as much whiskey furnished to the Indian and his friends

58

as they should ask for.   It was certainly a good stroke of business.   The victorious raiders did return that way, and Junction City was most hospitable to their thirst.   The valley of the Big Horn was resonant with their homeward yells.   They swept up the river, and the agent heard them coming, and he locked his door immediately.   He listened to their descent upon his fold, and he peeped out and saw them ride round the tightly shut buildings in their war-paint and the pride of utter success.   They had taken booty from the Piegans, and now, knocking at the store, they demanded ammunition, proclaiming at the same time in English that Cheschapah was a big man, and knew a "big heap medicine."   The agent told them from inside that they could not have any ammunition.   He also informed them that he knew who they were, and that they were under arrest.   This touched their primitive sense of the incongruous.   On the buoyancy of the whiskey they rode round and round the store containing the agent, and then rushed away, firing shots at the buildings and shots in the air, and so gloriously home among their tribe, while the agent sent a courier packing to Fort Custer.

The young bucks who had not gone on the raid to the Piegans thronged to hear the story, and the warriors told it here and there, walking in their feathers among a knot of friends, who listened with gay exclamations of pleasure and envy.   Great was Cheschapah, who had done all this !   And one and another told exactly and at length how he had seen the cold water rise into foam beneath the medicine-man's hand ; it could not be told too often ; not every companion of Cheschapah's had been accorded the privilege of witnessing this miracle, and each narrator in his circle became a wonder himself to the bold boy-ish faces that surrounded him. And after the miracle he told how the Piegans had been like a flock of birds before the medicine-man. Cheschapah himself passed among the groups, alone and aloof; he spoke to none, and he looked at none, and he noted how their voices fell to whispers as he passed; his ear caught the magic words of praise and awe; he felt the gaze of admiration follow him away, and a mist rose like incense in his brain. He wandered among the scattered tepees, and, turning, came along the same paths again, that he might once more overhear his worshippers. Great was Cheschapah! His heart beat, a throb of power passed through his body, and "Great is Cheschapah!" said he, aloud; for the fumes of hallucination wherewith he had drugged others had begun to make him drunk also. He sought a tepee where the wife of another chief was alone, and at his light call she stood at the entrance and heard him longer than she had ever listened to him before. But she withstood the temptation that was strong in the young chief's looks and words. She did not speak much, but laughed unsteadily, and, shaking her head with averted eyes, left him, and went where several women were together, and sat among them.

Cheschapah told his victory to the council, with many sentences about himself, and how his medicine had fended all hurt from the Crows. The elder chiefs sat cold.

"Ump!" said one, at the close of the oration, and "Heh!" remarked another. The sounds were of assent without surprise.

"It is good," said Pretty Eagle. His voice seemed to enrage Cheschapah.

60

"Heh! it is always pretty good!" remarked Spotted Horse.

"I have done this too," said Pounded Meat to his son, simply. "Once, twice, three times. The Crows have always been better warriors than the Piegans."

"Have you made water boil like me?" Cheschapah said.

"I am not a medicine-man," replied his father. "But I have taken horses and squaws from the Piegans. You make good medicine, maybe; but a cup of water will not kill many white men. Can you make the river boil? Let Cheschapah make bigger medicine, so the white man shall fear him as well as the Piegans, whose hearts are well known to us."

Cheschapah scowled. "Pounded Meat shall have this," said he. "I will make medicine to-morrow, old fool!"

"Drive him from the council!" said Pretty Eagle.

"Let him stay," said Pounded Meat. "His bad talk was not to the council, but to me, and I do not count it."

But the medicine-man left the presence of the chiefs, and came to the cabin of Kinney.

"Hello!" said the white man. "Sit down."

"You got that?" said the Indian, standing.

"More water medicine? I guess so. Take a seat."

"No, not boil any more. You got that other?"

"That other, eh? Well, now, you're not going to blind them yet? What's your hurry?"

"Yes. Make blind to-morrow. Me great chief!"

A slight uneasiness passed across the bantering face of Kinney. His Seltzer salts performed what he promised, but he had mentioned another miracle,

61

and he did not want his dupe to find him out until a war was thoroughly set agoing. He looked at the young Indian, noticing his eyes.

"What's the matter with you, anyway, Cheschapah?"

"Me great chief!" The raised voice trembled with unearthly conviction.

"Well, I guess you are. I guess you've got pretty far along," said the frontier cynic. He tilted his chair back and smiled at the child whose primitive brain he had tampered with so easily. The child stood looking at him with intent black eyes. "Better wait, Cheschapah. Come again. Medicine heap better after a while."

The Indian's quick ear caught the insincerity without understanding it. "You give me that quick!" he said, suddenly terrible.

"Oh, all right, Cheschapah. You know more medicine than me."

"Yes, I know more."

The white man brought a pot of scarlet paint, and the Indian's staring eyes contracted. Kinney took the battered cavalry sabre in his hand, and set its point in the earth floor of the cabin. "Stand back," he said, in mysterious tones, and Cheschapah shrank from the impending sorcery. Now Kinney had been to school once, in his Eastern childhood, and there had committed to memory portions of Shakespeare, Mrs. Hemans, and other poets out of a Reader. He had never forgotten a single word of any of them, and it now occurred to him that for the purposes of an incantation it would be both entertaining for himself and impressive to Cheschapah if he should recite "The Battle of Hohenlinden." He was drawing squares and circles with the point of the sabre.

"No," he said to himself, "that piece won't do. He knows too much English. Some of them words might strike him as bein' too usual, and he'd start to kill me, and spoil the whole thing. 'Munich' and 'chivalry' are snortin', but 'sun was low' ain't worth a damn. I guess—"

He stopped guessing, for the noon recess at school came in his mind, like a picture, and with it certain old-time preliminaries to the game of tag.

"' Eeny, meeny, money, my,' "

said Kinney, tapping himself, the sabre, the paint-pot, and Cheschapah in turn, one for each word. The incantation was begun. He held the sabre solemnly upright, while Cheschapah tried to control his excited breathing where he stood flattened against the wall.

"' Butter, leather, boney, stry ;
    Hare-bit, frost-neck,
    Harrico, barrico, whee, why, whoa, whack !'

You're it, Cheschapah." After that the weapon was given its fresh coat of paint, and Cheschapah went away with his new miracle in the dark.

"He is it," mused Kinney, grave, but inwardly lively. He was one of those sincere artists who need no popular commendation. "And whoever he does catch, it won't be me," he concluded. He felt pretty sure there would be war now.

Dawn showed the summoned troops near the agency at the corral, standing to horse. Cheschapah gathered his hostiles along the brow of the ridge in the rear of the agency buildings, and the two forces watched each other across the intervening four hundred yards.

"There they are," said the agent, jumping about. "Shoot them, colonel; shoot them!"

"You can't do that, you know," said the officer, "without an order from the President, or an overt act from the Indians."

So nothing happened, and Cheschapah told his friends the white men were already afraid of him. He saw more troops arrive, water their horses in the river, form line outside the corral, and dismount. He made ready at this movement, and all Indian on-lookers scattered from the expected fight. Yet the white man stayed quiet. It was issue day, but no families remained after drawing their rations. They had had no dance the night before, as was usual, and they did not linger a moment now, but came and departed with their beef and flour at once.

"I have done all this," said Cheschapah to Two Whistles.

"Cheschapah is a great man," assented the friend and follower. He had gone at once to his hay-field on his return from the Piegans, but some one had broken the little Indian's fence, and cattle were wandering in what remained of his crop.

"Our nation knows I will make a war, and therefore they do not stay here," said the medicine-man, caring nothing what Two Whistles might have suffered. "And now they will see that the white soldiers dare not fight with Cheschapah. The sun is high now, but they have not moved because I have stopped them. Do you not see it is my medicine?"

"We see it." It was the voice of the people.

But a chief spoke. "Maybe they wait for us to come."

Cheschapah answered. "Their eyes shall be made

64

sick. I will ride among them, but they will not know it." He galloped away alone, and lifted his red sword as he sped along the ridge of the hills, showing against the sky. Below at the corral the white soldiers waited ready, and heard him chanting his war song through the silence of the day. He turned in a long curve, and came in near the watching troops and through the agency, and then, made bolder by their motionless figures and guns held idle, he turned again and flew, singing, along close to the line, so they saw his eyes; and a few that had been talking low as they stood side by side fell silent at the spectacle. They could not shoot until some Indian should shoot. They watched him and the gray pony pass and return to the hostiles on the hill. Then they saw the hostiles melt away like magic. Their prophet had told them to go to their tepees and wait for the great rain he would now bring. It was noon, and the sky utterly blue over the bright valley. The sun rode a space nearer the west, and the thick black clouds assembled in the mountains and descended; their shadow flooded the valley with a lake of slatish blue, and presently the sudden torrents sluiced down with flashes and the ample thunder of Montana. Thus not alone the law against our soldiers firing the first shot in an Indian excitement, but now also the elements coincided to help the medicine-man's destiny.

Cheschapah sat in a tepee with his father, and as the rain splashed heavily on the earth the old man gazed at the young one.

"Why do you tremble, my son? You have made the white soldier's heart soft," said Pounded Meat. "You are indeed a great man, my son."

Cheschapah rose. "Do not call me your son,"

said he. "That is a lie." He went out into the fury of the rain, lifting his face against the drops, and exultingly calling out at each glare of the lightning. He went to Pretty Eagle's young squaw, who held off from him no longer, but got on a horse, and the two rode into the mountains. Before the sun had set, the sky was again utterly blue, and a cool scent rose everywhere in the shining valley.

The Crows came out of their tepees, and there were the white soldiers obeying orders and going away. They watched the column slowly move across the flat land below the bluffs, where the road led down the river twelve miles to the post.

"They are afraid," said new converts. "Cheschapah's rain has made their hearts soft."

"They have not all gone," said Pretty Eagle. "Maybe he did not make enough rain." But even Pretty Eagle began to be shaken, and he heard several of his brother chiefs during the next few days openly declare for the medicine-man. Cheschapah with his woman came from the mountains, and Pretty Eagle did not dare to harm him. Then another coincidence followed that was certainly most reassuring to the war party. Some of them had no meat, and told Cheschapah they were hungry. With consummate audacity he informed them he would give them plenty at once. On the same day another timely electric storm occurred up the river, and six steers were struck by lightning.

When the officers at Fort Custer heard of this they became serious.

"If this was not the nineteenth century," said Haines, "I should begin to think the elements were deliberately against us."

"It's very careless of the weather," said Stirling. "Very inconsiderate, at such a juncture."

Yet nothing more dangerous than red-tape happened for a while. There was an expensive quantity of investigation from Washington, and this gave the hostiles time to increase both in faith and numbers.

Among the excited Crows only a few wise old men held out. As for Cheschapah himself, ambition and success had brought him to the weird enthusiasm of a fanatic. He was still a charlatan, but a charlatan who believed utterly in his star. He moved among his people with growing mystery, and his hapless adjutant, Two Whistles, rode with him, slaved for him, abandoned the plans he had for making himself a farm, and, desiring peace in his heart, weakly cast his lot with war. Then one day there came an order from the agent to all the Indians : they were to come in by a certain fixed day. The department commander had assembled six hundred troops at the post, and these moved up the river and went into camp. The usually empty ridges, and the bottom where the road ran, filled with white and red men. Half a mile to the north of the buildings, on the first rise from the river, lay the cavalry, and some infantry above them with a howitzer, while across the level, three hundred yards opposite, along the river-bank, was the main Indian camp. Even the hostiles had obeyed the agent's order, and came in close to the troops, totally unlike hostiles in general ; for Cheschapah had told them he would protect them with his medicine, and they shouted and sang all through this last night. The women joined with harsh cries and shriekings, and a scalp-dance went on, besides lesser commotions and gatherings, with the throbbing of drums every-

67

where. Through the sleepless din ran the barking of a hundred dogs, that herded and hurried in crowds of twenty at a time, meeting, crossing from fire to fire among the tepees. Their yelps rose to the high bench of land, summoning a horde of coyotes. These cringing nomads gathered from the desert in a tramp army, and, skulking down the bluffs, sat in their outer darkness and ceaselessly howled their long, shrill greeting to the dogs that sat in the circle of light. The general sent scouts to find the nature of the dance and hubbub, and these brought word it was peaceful; and in the morning another scout summoned the elder chiefs to a talk with the friend who had come from the Great Father at Washington to see them and find if their hearts were good.

"Our hearts are good," said Pretty Eagle. "We do not want war. If you want Cheschapah, we will drive him out from the Crows to you."

"There are other young chiefs with bad hearts," said the commissioner, naming the ringleaders that were known. He made a speech, but Pretty Eagle grew sullen. "It is well," said the commissioner; "you will not help me to make things smooth, and now I step aside and the war chief will talk."

"If you want any other chiefs," said Rretty Eagle, "come and take them."

"Pretty Eagle shall have an hour and a half to think on my words," said the general. "I have plenty of men behind me to make my words good. You must send me all those Indians who fired at the agency."

The Crow chiefs returned to the council, which was apart from the war party's camp; and Cheschapah walked in among them, and after him, slowly, old Pound-ed Meat, to learn how the conference had gone.

68

"You have made a long talk with the white man," said Cheschapah. "Talk is pretty good for old men. I and the young chiefs will fight now and kill our enemies."

"Cheschapah," said Pounded Meat, "if your medicine is good, it may be the young chiefs will kill our enemies to-day. But there are other days to come, and after them still others; there are many, many days. My son, the years are a long road. The life of one man is not long, but enough to learn this thing truly: the white man will always return. There was a day on this river when the dead soldiers of Yellow Hair lay in hills, and the squaws of the Sioux warriors climbed among them with their knives. What do the Sioux warriors do now when they meet the white man on this river? Their hearts are on the ground, and they go home like children when the white man says, 'You shall not visit your friends.' My son, I thought war was good once. I have kept you from the arrows of our enemies on many trails when you were so little that my blankets were enough for both. Your mother was not here any more, and the chiefs laughed because I carried you. Oh, my son, I have seen the hearts of the Sioux broken by the white man, and I do not think war is good."

"The talk of Pounded Meat is very good," said Pretty Eagle. "If Cheschapah were wise like his father, this trouble would not have come to the Crows. But we could not give the white chief so many of our chiefs that he asked for to day."

Cheschapah laughed. "Did he ask for so many? He wanted only Cheschapah, who is not wise like Pounded Meat."

"You would have been given to him," said Pretty Eagle.

69

"Did Pretty Eagle tell the white chief that? Did he say he would give Cheschapah? How would he give me? In one hand, or two? Or would the old warrior take me to the white man's camp on the horse his young squaw left?"

Pretty Eagle raised his rifle, and Pounded Meat, quick as a boy, seized the barrel and pointed it up among the poles of the tepee, where the quiet black fire smoke was oozing out into the air. "Have you lived so long," said Pounded Meat to his ancient comrade, "and do this in the council?" His wrinkled head and hands shook, the sudden strength left him, and the rifle fell free.

"Let Pretty Eagle shoot," said Cheschapah, looking at the council. He stood calm, and the seated chiefs turned their grim eyes upon him. Certainty was in his face, and doubt in theirs. "Let him send his bullet five times—ten times. Then I will go and let the white soldiers shoot at me until they all lie dead."

"It is heavy for me," began Pounded Meat, "that my friend should be the enemy of my son."

"Tell that lie no more," said Cheschapah. "You are not my father. I have made the white man blind, and I have softened his heart with the rain. I will call the rain to-day." He raised his red sword, and there was a movement among the sitting figures. "The clouds will come from my father's place, where I have talked with him as one chief to another. My mother went into the mountains to gather berries. She was young, and the thunder-maker saw her face. He brought the black clouds, so her feet turned from home, and she walked where the river goes into the great walls of the mountain, and that day she was stricken fruitful by the lightning. You are not the

70

father of Cheschapah." He dealt Pounded Meat a blow, and the old man fell. But the council sat still until the sound of Cheschapah's galloping horse died away. They were ready now to risk everything. Their scepticism was conquered.

The medicine-man galloped to his camp of hostiles, and, seeing him, they yelled and quickly finished plaiting their horses' tails. Cheschapah had accomplished his wish; he had become the prophet of all the Crows, and he led the armies of the faithful. Each man stripped his blanket off and painted his body for the fight. The forms slipped in and out of the brush, buckling their cartridge-belts, bringing their ponies, while many families struck their tepees and moved up nearer the agency. The spare horses were run across the river into the hills, and through the yelling that shifted and swept like flames along the wind the hostiles made ready and gathered, their crowds quivering with motion, and changing place and shape as more mounted Indians appeared.

"Are the holes dug deep as I marked them on the earth?" said Cheschapah to Two Whistles. "That is good. We shall soon have to go into them from the great rain I will bring. Make these strong, to stay as we ride. They are good medicine, and with them the white soldiers will not see you any more than they saw me when I rode among them that day."

He had strips and capes of red flannel, and he and Two Whistles fastened them to their painted bodies.

"You will let me go with you?" said Two Whistles.

"You are my best friend," said Cheschapah, "and to-day I will take you. You shall see my great medicine when I make the white man's eyes grow sick."

The two rode forward, and one hundred and fifty

71

followed them, bursting from their tepees like an explosion, and rushing along quickly in skirmish-line. Two Whistles rode beside his speeding prophet, and saw the red sword waving near his face, and the sun in the great still sky, and the swimming, fleeting earth. His superstition and the fierce ride put him in a sort of trance.

" The medicine is beginning !" shouted Cheschapah ; and at that Two Whistles saw the day grow large with terrible shining, and heard his own voice calling and could not stop it. They left the hundred and fifty behind, he knew not where or when. He saw the line of troops ahead change to separate waiting shapes of men, and their legs and arms become plain ; then all the guns took clear form in lines of steady glitter. He seemed suddenly alone far ahead of the band, but the voice of Cheschapah spoke close by his ear through the singing wind, and he repeated each word without understanding ; he was watching the ground rush by, lest it might rise against his face, and all the while he felt his horse's motion under him, smooth and perpetual. Something weighed against his leg, and there was Cheschapah he had forgotten, always there at his side, veering him around somewhere. But there was no red sword waving. Then the white men must be blind already, wherever they were, and Cheschapah, the only thing he could see, sat leaning one hand on his horse's rump firing a pistol. The ground came swimming towards his eyes always, smooth and wide like a gray flood, but Two Whistles knew that Cheschapah would not let it sweep him away. He saw a horse without a rider floated out of blue smoke, and floated in again with a cracking noise ; white soldiers moved in a row across his eyes, very small and clear, and broke into a blurred eddy of shapes which the flood swept away clean and empty. Then a dead white man came by on the quick flood. Two Whistles saw the yellow stripe on his sleeve; but he was gone, and there was nothing but sky and blaze, with Cheschapah's head-dress in the middle. The horse's even motion continued beneath him, when suddenly the head-dress fell out of Two Whistles' sight, and the earth returned. They were in brush, with his horse standing and breathing, and a dead horse on the ground with Cheschapah, and smoke and moving people everywhere outside. He saw Cheschapah run from the dead horse and jump on a gray pony and go. Somehow he was on the ground too, looking at a red sword lying beside his face. He stared at it a long while, then took it in his hand, still staring; all at once he rose and broke it savagely, and fell again. His faith was shivered to pieces like glass. But he got on his horse, and the horse moved away. He was looking at the blood running on his body. The horse moved always, and Two Whistles followed with his eye a little deeper gush of blood along a crease in his painted skin, noticed the flannel, and remembering the lie of his prophet, instantly began tearing the red rags from his body, and flinging them to the ground with cries of scorn. Presently he heard some voices, and soon one voice much nearer, and saw he had come to a new place, where there were white soldiers looking at him quietly. One was riding up and telling him to give up his pistol. Two Whistles got off and stood behind his horse, looking at the pistol. The white soldier came quite near, and at his voice Two Whistles moved slowly out from behind the horse, and listened to the cool words as the soldier repeated his command.

The Indian was pointing his pistol uncertainly, and he looked at the soldier's coat and buttons, and the straps on the shoulders, and the bright steel sabre, and the white man's blue eyes; then Two Whistles looked at his own naked, clotted body, and, turning the pistol against himself, fired it into his breast.

Far away up the river, on the right of the line, a lieutenant with two men was wading across after some hostiles that had been skirmishing with his troop. The hostiles had fallen back after some hot shooting, and had dispersed among the brush and tepees on the farther shore, picking up their dead, as Indians do. It was interesting work, this splashing breast-high through a river into a concealed hornets'-nest, and the lieutenant thought a little on his unfinished plans and duties in life; he noted one dead Indian left on the shore, and went steadfastly in among the half-seen tepees, rummaging and beating in the thick brush to be sure no hornets remained. Finding them gone, and their dead spirited away, he came back on the bank to the one dead Indian, who had a fine head-dress, and was still ribanded with gay red streamers of flannel, and was worth all the rest of the dead put together, and much more. The head lay in the water, and one hand held the rope of the gray pony, who stood quiet and uninterested over his fallen rider. They began carrying the prize across to the other bank, where many had now collected, among others Kinney and the lieutenant's captain, who subsequently said, " I found the body of Cheschapah ;" and, indeed, it was a very good thing to be able to say.

" This busts the war," said Kinney to the captain, as the body was being lifted over the Little Horn. " They know he's killed, and they've all quit. I was up by the tepees near the agency just now, and I could see the hostiles jamming back home for dear life. They was chucking their rifles to the squaws, and jumping in the river—ha! ha!—to wash off their war-paint, and each ——— ——— would crawl out and sit innercint in the family blanket his squaw had ready. If you was to go there now, cap'n, you'd find just a lot of harmless Injuns eatin' supper like all the year round. Let me help you, boys, with that carcass."

Kinney gave a hand to the lieutenant and men of G troop, First United States Cavalry, and they lifted Cheschapah up the bank. In the tilted position of the body the cartridge-belt slid a little, and a lump of newspaper fell into the stream. Kinney watched it open and float away with a momentary effervescence. The dead medicine-man was laid between the white and red camps, that all might see he could be killed like other people; and this wholesome discovery brought the Crows to terms at once. Pretty Eagle had displayed a flag of truce, and now he surrendered the guilty chiefs whose hearts had been bad. Every one came where the dead prophet lay to get a look at him. For a space of hours Pretty Eagle and the many other Crows he had deceived rode by in single file, striking him with their whips; after them came a young squaw, and she also lashed the upturned face.

This night was untroubled at the agency, and both camps and the valley lay quiet in the peaceful dark. Only Pounded Meat, alone on the top of a hill, mourned for his son; and his wailing voice sounded through the silence until the new day came. Then the general had him stopped and brought in, for it might be that the old man's noise would unsettle the Crows again.

75

The Second Missouri Compromise

I

THE Legislature had sat up all night, much absorbed, having taken off its coat because of the stove. This was the fortieth and final day of its first session under an order of things not new only, but novel. It sat with the retrospect of forty days' duty done, and the prospect of forty days' consequent pay to come. Sleepy it was not, but wide and wider awake over a progressing crisis. Hungry it had been until after a breakfast fetched to it from the Overland at seven, three hours ago. It had taken no intermission to wash its face, nor was there just now any apparatus for this, as the tin pitcher commonly used stood not in the basin in the corner, but on the floor by the Governor's chair; so the eyes of the Legislature, though earnest, were dilapidated. Last night the pressure of public business had seemed over, and no turning back the hands of the clock likely to be necessary. Besides Governor Ballard, Mr. Hewley, Secretary and Treasurer, was sitting up too, small, iron-gray, in feature and bearing every inch the capable, dignified official, but his necktie had slipped off during the night. The bearded Councillors had the best of it, seeming after their vigil less stale in the face than the member from Silver City, for instance, whose day-old black growth blurred his dingy chin, or the member from Big Camas, whose scantier red crop bristled on his cheeks in sparse wandering arrangements, like spikes on the barrel of a musical box. For comfort, most of the pistols were on the table with the Statutes of the United States. Secretary and Treasurer Hewley's lay on his strong-box immediately behind him. The Governor's was a light one, and always hung in the armhole of his waistcoat. The graveyard of Boisé City this year had twenty-seven tenants, two brought there by meningitis, and twenty-five by difference of opinion. Many denizens of the Territory were miners, and the unsettling element of gold-dust hung in the air, breeding argument. The early, thin, bright morning steadily mellowed against the windows distant from the stove; the panes melted clear until they ran, steamed faintly, and dried, this fresh May day, after the night's untimely cold; while still the Legislature sat in its shirt-sleeves, and several statesmen had removed their boots. Even had appearances counted, the session was invisible from the street. Unlike a good number of houses in the town, the State-House (as they called it from old habit) was not all on the ground-floor for outsiders to stare into, but up a flight of wood steps to a wood gallery. From this, to be sure, the interior could be watched from several windows on both sides; but the journey up the steps was precisely enough to disincline the idle, and this was counted a sensible thing by the lawmakers. They took the ground that shaping any government for a raw wilderness community needed seclusion, and they set a high value upon unworried privacy.

The sun had set upon a concentrated Council, but it rose upon faces that looked momentous. Only the Governor's and Treasurer's were impassive, and they concealed something even graver than the matter in hand.

"I'll take a hun'red mo', Gove'nuh," said the member from Silver City, softly, his eyes on space. His name was Powhattan Wingo.

The Governor counted out the blue, white, and red chips to Wingo, pencilled some figures on a thickly ciphered and cancelled paper that bore in print the words "Territory of Idaho, Council Chamber," and then filled up his glass from the tin pitcher, adding a little sugar.

"And I'll trouble you fo' the toddy," Wingo added, always softly, and his eyes always on space. "Raise you ten, suh." This was to the Treasurer. Only the two were playing at present. The Governor was kindly acting as bank ; the others were looking on.

"And ten," said the Treasurer.

"And ten," said Wingo.

"And twenty," said the Treasurer.

"And fifty," said Wingo, gently bestowing his chips in the middle of the table.

The Treasurer called.

The member from Silver City showed down five high hearts, and a light rustle went over the Legislature when the Treasurer displayed three twos and a pair of threes, and gathered in his harvest. He had drawn two cards, Wingo one ; and losing to the lowest hand that could have beaten you is under such circumstances truly hard luck. Moreover, it was almost the only sort of luck that had attended Wingo since about half after three that morning. Seven hours of

81

cards just a little lower than your neighbor's is searching to the nerves.

"Gove'nuh, I'll take a hun'red mo'," said Wingo; and once again the Legislature rustled lightly, and the new deal began.

Treasurer Hewley's winnings flanked his right, a pillared fortress on the table, built chiefly of Wingo's misfortunes. Hewley had not counted them, and his architecture was for neatness and not ostentation; yet the Legislature watched him arrange his gains with sullen eyes. It would have pleased him now to lose; it would have more than pleased him to be able to go to bed quite a long time ago. But winners cannot easily go to bed. The thoughtful Treasurer bet his money and deplored this luck. It seemed likely to trap himself and the Governor in a predicament they had not foreseen. All had taken a hand at first, and played for several hours, until Fortune's wheel ran into a rut deeper than usual. Wingo slowly became the loser to several, then Hewley had forged ahead, winner from everybody. One by one they had dropped out, each meaning to go home, and all lingering to see the luck turn. It was an extraordinary run, a rare specimen, a breaker of records, something to refer to in the future as a standard of measure and an embellishment of reminiscence; quite enough to keep the Idaho Legislature up all night. And then it was their friend who was losing. The only speaking in the room was the brief card talk of the two players.

"Five better," said Hewley, winner again four times in the last five.

"Ten," said Wingo.

"And twenty," said the Secretary and Treasurer.

"Call you."

"Three kings."

"They are good, suh. Gove'nuh, I'll take a hun-'red mo'."

Upon this the wealthy and weary Treasurer made a try for liberty and bed. How would it do, he suggested, to have a round of jack-pots, say ten—or twenty, if the member from Silver City preferred—and then stop? It would do excellently, the member said, so softly that the Governor looked at him. But Wingo's large countenance remained inexpressive, his black eyes still impersonally fixed on space. He sat thus till his chips were counted to him, and then the eyes moved to watch the cards fall. The Governor hoped he might win now, under the jack-pot system. At noon he should have a disclosure to make ; something that would need the most cheerful and contented feelings in Wingo and the Legislature to be received with any sort of calm. Wingo was behind the game to the tune of—the Governor gave up adding as he ran his eye over the figures of the bank's erased and tormented record, and he shook his head to himself. This was inadvertent.

"May I inquah who yo're shakin' yoh head at, suh ?" said Wingo, wheeling upon the surprised Governor.

"Certainly," answered that official. "You." He was never surprised for very long. In 1867 it did not do to remain surprised in Idaho.

"And have I done anything which meets yoh disapprobation ?" pursued the member from Silver City, enunciating with care.

"You have met my disapprobation."

Wingo's eye was on the Governor, and now his friends drew a little together, and as a unit sent a glance of suspicion at the lone bank.

"You will gratify me by being explicit, suh," said Wingo to the bank.

"Well, you've emptied the toddy."

"Ha-ha, Gove'nuh! I rose, suh, to yoh little fly. We'll awduh some mo'."

"Time enough when he comes for the breakfast things," said Governor Ballard, easily.

"As you say, suh. I'll open for five dolluhs." Wingo turned back to his game. He was winning, and as his luck continued his voice ceased to be soft, and became a shade truculent. The Governor's ears caught this change, and he also noted the lurking triumph in the faces of Wingo's fellow-statesmen. Cheerfulness and content were scarcely reigning yet in the Council Chamber of Idaho as Ballard sat watching the friendly game. He was beginning to fear that he must leave the Treasurer alone and take some precautions outside. But he would have to be separated for some time from his ally, cut off from giving him any hints. Once the Treasurer looked at him, and he immediately winked reassuringly, but the Treasurer failed to respond. Hewley might be able to wink after everything was over, but he could not find it in his serious heart to do so now. He was wondering what would happen if this game should last till noon with the company in its present mood. Noon was the time fixed for paying the Legislative Assembly the compensation due for its services during this session; and the Governor and the Treasurer had put their heads together and arranged a surprise for the Legislative Assembly. They were not going to pay them.

A knock sounded at the door, and on seeing the waiter from the Overland enter, the Governor was seized with an idea. Perhaps precaution could be taken from the inside. "Take this pitcher," said he, "and have it refilled with the same. Joseph knows my mixture." But Joseph was night bar-tender, and now long in his happy bed, with a day successor in the saloon, and this one did not know the mixture. Ballard had foreseen this when he spoke, and that his writing a note of directions would seem quite natural.

"The receipt is as long as the drink," said a legislator, watching the Governor's pencil fly.

"He don't know where my private stock is located," explained Ballard. The waiter departed with the breakfast things and the note, and while the jackpots continued the Governor's mind went carefully over the situation.

Until lately the Western citizen has known one every-day experience that no dweller in our thirteen original colonies has had for two hundred years. In Massachusetts they have not seen it since 1641; in Virginia not since 1628. It is that of belonging to a community of which every adult was born somewhere else. When you come to think of this a little it is dislocating to many of your conventions. Let a citizen of Salem, for instance, or a well-established Philadelphia Quaker, try to imagine his chief-justice fresh from Louisiana, his mayor from Arkansas, his tax-collector from South Carolina, and himself recently arrived in a wagon from a thousand-mile drive. To be governor of such a community Ballard had travelled in a wagon from one quarter of the horizon; from another quarter Wingo had arrived on a mule. People reached Boisé in three ways: by rail to a little west of the Missouri, after which it was wagon, saddle, or

85

walk for the remaining fifteen hundred miles ; from California it was shorter; and from Portland, Oregon, only about five hundred miles, and some of these more agreeable, by water up the Columbia. Thus it happened that salt often sold for its weight in gold-dust. A miner in the Bannock Basin would meet a freight teamster coming in with the staples of life, having journeyed perhaps sixty consecutive days through the desert, and valuing his salt highly. The two accordingly bartered in scales, white powder against yellow, and both parties content. Some in Boisé to-day can remember these bargains. After all, they were struck but thirty years ago. Governor Ballard and Treasurer Hewley did not come from the same place, but they constituted a minority of two in Territorial politics because they hailed from north of Mason and Dixon's line. Powhattan Wingo and the rest of the Council were from Pike County, Missouri. They had been Secessionists, some of them Knights of the Golden Circle ; they had belonged to Price's Left Wing, and they flocked together. They were seven—two lying unwell at the Overland, five now present in the State-House with the Governor and Treasurer. Wingo, Gascon Claiborne, Gratiot des Pères, Pete Cawthon, and F. Jackson Gilet were their names. Besides this Council of seven were thirteen members of the Idaho House of Representatives, mostly of the same political feather with the Council, and they too would be present at noon to receive their pay. How Ballard and Hewley came to be a minority of two is a simple matter. Only twenty-five months had gone since Appomattox Court-House. That surrender was presently followed by Johnston's to Sherman, at Durhams Station, and following this

86

the various Confederate armies in Alabama, or across
the Mississippi, or wherever they happened to be, had
successively surrendered—but not Price's Left Wing.
There was the wide open West under its nose, and no
Grant or Sherman infesting that void. Why surrender? Wingos, Claibornes, and all, they melted away.
Price's Left Wing sailed into the prairie and passed
below the horizon. To know what it next did you
must, like Ballard or Hewley, pass below the horizon
yourself, clean out of sight of the dome at Washington
to remote, untracked Idaho. There, besides wild red
men in quantities, would you find not very tame white
ones, gentlemen of the ripest Southwestern persua-
sion, and a Legislature to fit. And if, like Ballard or
Hewley, you were a Union man, and the President of
the United States had appointed you Governor or
Secretary of such a place, your days would be full of
awkwardness, though your difference in creed might
not hinder you from playing draw-poker with the un-
reconstructed. These Missourians were whole-souled,
ample-natured males in many ways, but born with a
habit of hasty shooting. The Governor, on setting
foot in Idaho, had begun to study pistolship, but ac-
quired thus in middle life it could never be with him
that spontaneous art which it was with Price's Left
Wing. Not that the weapons now lying loose about
the State-House were brought for use there. Everybody always went armed in Boisé, as the gravestones
impliedly testified. Still, the thought of the bad quarter of an hour which it might come to at noon did
cross Ballard's mind, raising the image of a column
in the morrow's paper: "An unfortunate occurrence
has ended relations between esteemed gentlemen
hitherto the warmest personal friends. . . . They will

87

be laid to rest at 3 P.M. . . . As a last token of respect for our lamented Governor, the troops from
Boisé Barracks. . . ." The Governor trusted that if
his friends at the post were to do him any service it
would not be a funeral one.

The new pitcher of toddy came from the Overland,
the jack-pots continued, were nearing a finish, and
Ballard began to wonder if anything had befallen a
part of his note to the bar-tender, an enclosure addressed to another person.

"Ha, suh!" said Wingo to Hewley. "My pot
again, I declah." The chips had been crossing the
table his way, and he was now loser but six hundred
dollars.

"Ye ain't goin' to whip Mizzooruh all night an' all
day, ez a rule," observed Pete Cawthon, Councillor
from Lost Leg.

"'Tis a long road that has no turnin', Gove'nuh,"
said F. Jackson Gilet, more urbanely. He had been
in public life in Missouri, and was now President of
the Council in Idaho. He, too, had arrived on a
mule, but could at will summon a rhetoric dating from
Cicero, and preserved by many luxuriant orators until after the middle of the present century.

"True," said the Governor, politely. "But here
sits the long suffering bank, whichever way the road
turns. "I'm sleepy."

"You sacrifice yo'self in the good cause," replied
Gilet, pointing to the poker game. "Oneasy lies the
head that wahs an office, suh." And Gilet bowed
over his compliment.

The Governor thought so indeed. He looked at the
Treasurer's strong-box, where lay the appropriation
lately made by Congress to pay the Idaho Legislature

88

for its services; and he looked at the Treasurer, in whose pocket lay the key of the strong-box. He was accountable to the Treasury at Washington for all money disbursed for Territorial expenses.

"Eleven twenty," said Wingo, "and only two hands mo' to play."

The Governor slid out his own watch.

"I'll scahsely recoup," said Wingo.

They dealt and played the hand, and the Governor strolled to the window.

"Three aces," Wingo announced, winning again handsomely. "I struck my luck too late," he commented to the on-lookers. While losing he had been able to sustain a smooth reticence; now he gave his thoughts freely to the company, and continually moved and fingered his increasing chips. The Governor was still looking out of the window, where he could see far up the street, when Wingo won the last hand, which was small. "That ends it, suh, I suppose?" he said to Hewley, letting the pack of cards linger in his grasp.

"I wouldn't let him off yet," said Ballard to Wingo from the window, with sudden joviality, and he came back to the players. "I'd make him throw five cold hands with me."

"Ah, Gove'nuh, that's yoh spo'tin' blood! Will you do it, Mistuh Hewley—a hun'red a hand?"

Mr. Hewley did it; and winning the first, he lost the second, third, and fourth in the space of an eager minute, while the Councillors drew their chairs close.

"Let me see," said Wingo, calculating, "if I lose this—why still—" He lost. "But I'll not have to ask you to accept my papuh, suh. Wingo liquidates. Fo'ty days at six dolluhs a day makes six times fo' is

89

twenty-fo'—two hun'red an' fo'ty dolluhs spot cash in hand at noon, without computation of mileage to and from Silver City at fo' dolluhs every twenty miles, estimated according to the nearest usually travelled route." He was reciting part of the statute providing mileage for Idaho legislators. He had never served the public before, and he knew all the laws concerning compensation by heart. "You'll not have to wait fo' yoh money, suh," he concluded.

"Well, Mr. Wingo," said Governor Ballard, "it depends on yourself whether your pay comes to you or not." He spoke cheerily. "If you don't see things my way, our Treasurer will have to wait for his money." He had not expected to break the news just so, but it made as easy a beginning as any.

"See things yoh way, suh?"

"Yes. As it stands at present I cannot take the responsibility of paying you."

"The United States pays me, suh. My compensation is provided by act of Congress."

"I confess I am unable to discern your responsibility, Gove'nuh," said F. Jackson Gilet. "Mr. Wingo has faithfully attended the session, and is, like every gentleman present, legally entitled to his emoluments."

"You can all readily become entitled—"

"All? Am I — are my friends — included in this new depa'tyuh?"

"The difficulty applies generally, Mr. Gilet."

"Do I understand the Gove'nuh to insinuate—nay, gentlemen, do not rise! Be seated, I beg." For the Councillors had leaped to their feet.

"Whar's our money?" said Pete Cawthon. "Our money was put in thet yere box."

90

Ballard flushed angrily, but a knock at the door stopped him, and he merely said, " Come in."

A trooper, a corporal, stood at the entrance, and the disordered Council endeavored to look usual in a stranger's presence. They resumed their seats, but it was not easy to look usual on such short notice.

" Captain Paisley's compliments," said the soldier, mechanically, " and will Governor Ballard take supper with him this evening?"

" Thank Captain Paisley," said the Governor (his tone was quite usual), " and say that official business connected with the end of the session makes it imperative for me to be at the State-House. Imperative."

The trooper withdrew. He was a heavy-built, handsome fellow, with black mustache and black eyes that watched through two straight, narrow slits beneath straight black brows. His expression in the Council Chamber had been of the regulation military indifference, and as he went down the steps he irrelevantly sang an old English tune :

" 'Since first I saw your face I resolved
    To honor and re—'

I guess," he interrupted himself as he unhitched his horse, " parrot and monkey hev broke loose."

The Legislature, always in its shirt - sleeves, the cards on the table, and the toddy on the floor, sat calm a moment, cooled by this brief pause from the first heat of its surprise, while the clatter of Corporal Jones's galloping shrank quickly into silence.

Captain Paisley walked slowly from the adjutant's office at Boisé Barracks to his quarters, and his orderly walked behind him. The captain carried a letter in his hand, and the orderly, though distant a respectful ten paces, could hear him swearing plain as day. When he reached his front door Mrs. Paisley met him.

"Jim," cried she, "two more chickens froze in the night." And the delighted orderly heard the captain so plainly that he had to blow his nose or burst.

The lady, merely remarking "My goodness, Jim," retired immediately to the kitchen, where she had a soldier cook baking, and feared he was not quite sober enough to do it alone. The captain had paid eighty dollars for forty hens this year at Boisé, and twenty-nine had now passed away, victims to the climate. His wise wife perceived his extreme language not to have been all on account of hens, however; but he never allowed her to share in his professional worries, so she stayed safe with the baking, and he sat in the front room with a cigar in his mouth.

Boisé was a two-company post without a major, and Paisley, being senior captain, was in command, an office to which he did not object. But his duties so far this month of May had not pleased him in the least. Theoretically, you can have at a two-company post the following responsible people: one major, two captains, four lieutenants, a doctor, and a chaplain. The major has been spoken of; it is almost needless to say that the chaplain was on leave, and had never been seen at Boisé by any of the present garrison; two of the lieutenants were also on leave, and two on surveying details—they had influence at Washington; the other captain was on a scout with General Crook somewhere near the Malheur Agency, and the doctor had only arrived this week. There had resulted a period when Captain Paisley was his own adjutant, quartermaster, and post surgeon, with not even an efficient sergeant to rely upon; and during this period his wife had stayed a good deal in the kitchen. Happily the doctor's coming had given relief to the hospital steward and several patients, and to the captain not only an equal, but an old friend, with whom to pour out his disgust; and together every evening they freely expressed their opinion of the War Department and its treatment of the Western army.

There were steps at the door, and Paisley hurried out. "Only you!" he exclaimed, with such frank vexation that the doctor laughed loudly. "Come in, man, come in," Paisley continued, leading him strongly by the arm, sitting him down, and giving him a cigar. "Here's a pretty how de do!"

"More Indians!" inquired Dr. Tuck.

"Bother! they're nothing. It's Senators—Councillors—whatever the Territorial devils call themselves."

"Gone on the war-path?" the doctor said, quite ignorant how nearly he had touched the Council.

"Precisely, man. War-path. Here's the Governor writing me they'll be scalping him in the State-House at twelve o'clock. It's past 11.30. They'll be whetting knives about now." And the captain roared.

"I know you haven't gone crazy," said the doctor, "but who has?"

"The lot of them. Ballard's a good man, and—

93

what's his name?—the little Secretary. The balance are just mad dogs—mad dogs. Look here: 'Dear Captain'—that's Ballard to me. I just got it—'I find myself unexpectedly hampered this morning. The South shows signs of being too solid. Unless I am supported, my plan for bringing our Legislature to terms will have to be postponed. Hewley and I are more likely to be brought to terms ourselves—a bad precedent to establish in Idaho. Noon is the hour for drawing salaries. Ask me to supper as quick as you can, and act on my reply.' I've asked him," continued Paisley, "but I haven't told Mrs. Paisley to cook anything extra yet." The captain paused to roar again, shaking Tuck's shoulder for sympathy. Then he explained the situation in Idaho to the justly bewildered doctor. Ballard had confided many of his difficulties lately to Paisley.

"He means you're to send troops?" Tuck inquired.

"What else should the poor man mean?"

"Are you sure it's constitutional?"

"Hang constitutional! What do I know about their legal quibbles at Washington?"

"But, Paisley—"

"They're unsurrendered rebels, I tell you. Never signed a parole."

"But the general amnesty—"

"Bother general amnesty! Ballard represents the Federal government in this Territory, and Uncle Sam's army is here to protect the Federal government. If Ballard calls on the army it's our business to obey, and if there's any mistake in judgment it's Ballard's, not mine." Which was sound soldier common-sense, and happened to be equally good law. This is not always the case.

94

"You haven't got any force to send," said Tuck.

This was true. General Crook had taken with him both Captain Sinclair's infantry and the troop (or company, as cavalry was also then called) of the First.

"A detail of five or six with a reliable non-commissioned officer will do to remind them it's the United States they're bucking against," said Paisley. "There's a deal in the moral of these things. Crook—" Paisley broke off and ran to the door. "Hold his horse!" he called out to the orderly; for he had heard the hoofs, and was out of the house before Corporal Jones had fairly arrived. So Jones sprang off and hurried up, saluting. He delivered his message.

"Um—umpra—what's that? Is it *imperative* you mean?" suggested Paisley.

"Yes, sir," said Jones, reforming his pronunciation of that unaccustomed word. "He said it twiced."

"What were they doing?"

"Blamed if I—beg the captain's pardon—they looked like they was waitin' fer me to git out."

"Go on—go on. How many were there?"

"Seven, sir. There was Governor Ballard and Mr. Hewley and—well, them's all the names I know. But," Jones hastened on with eagerness, "I've saw them five other fellows before at a—at—" The corporal's voice failed, and he stood looking at the captain.

"Well? Where?"

"At a cock-fight, sir," murmured Jones, casting his eyes down.

A slight sound came from the room where Tuck was seated, listening, and Paisley's round gray eyes

95

rolled once, then steadied themselves fiercely upon Jones.

"Did you notice anything further unusual, corporal?"

"No, sir, except they was excited in there. Looked like they might be goin' to hev considerable rough house—a fuss, I mean, sir. Two was in their socks. I counted four guns on a table."

"Take five men and go at once to the State-House. If the Governor needs assistance you will give it, but do nothing hasty. Stop trouble, and make none. You've got twenty minutes."

"Captain—if anybody needs arrestin'—"

"You must be judge of that." Paisley went into the house. There was no time for particulars.

"Snakes!" remarked Jones. He jumped on his horse and dashed down the slope to the men's quarters.

"Crook may be here any day or any hour," said Paisley, returning to the doctor. "With two companies in the background, I think Price's Left Wing will subside this morning."

"Supposing they don't?"

"I'll go myself; and when it gets to Washington that the commanding officer at Boisé personally interfered with the Legislature of Idaho, it 'll shock 'em to that extent that the government will have to pay for a special commission of investigation and two tons of red tape. I've got to trust to that corporal's good sense. I haven't another man at the post."

Corporal Jones had three-quarters of a mile to go, and it was ten minutes before noon, so he started his five men at a run. His plan was to walk and look quiet as soon as he reached the town, and thus excite

96

no curiosity. The citizens were accustomed to the sight of passing soldiers. Jones had thought out several things, and he was not going to order bayonets fixed until the final necessary moment. "Stop trouble and make none" was firm in his mind. He had not long been a corporal. It was still his first enlistment. His habits were by no means exemplary; and his frontier personality, strongly developed by six years of vagabonding before he enlisted, was scarcely yet disciplined into the military machine of the regulation pattern that it should and must become before he could be counted a model soldier. His captain had promoted him to steady him, if that could be, and to give his better qualities a chance. Since then he had never been drunk at the wrong time. Two years ago it would not have entered his free-lance heart to be reticent with any man, high or low, about any pleasure in which he saw fit to indulge; to-day he had been shy over confessing to the commanding officer his leaning to cock-fights—a sign of his approach to the correct mental attitude of the enlisted man. Being corporal had wakened in him a new instinct, and this State-House affair was the first chance he had had to show himself. He gave the order to proceed at a walk in such a tone that one of the troopers whispered to another, "Specimen ain't going to forget he's wearing a chevron."

III

THE brief silence that Jones and his invitation to supper had caused among the Councillors was first broken by F. Jackson Gilet.

"Gentlemen," he said, "as President of the Council

97

I rejoice in an interruption that has given pause to our haste and saved us from ill-considered expressions of opinion. The Gove'nuh has, I confess, surprised me. Befo' examining the legal aspect of our case I will ask the Gove'nuh if he is familiar with the sundry statutes applicable."

"I think so," Ballard replied, pleasantly.

"I had supposed," continued the President of the Council—"nay, I had congratulated myself that our weightiuh tasks of law-making and so fo'th were consummated yesterday, our thirty-ninth day, and that our friendly game of last night would be, as it were, the finis that crowned with pleashuh the work of a session memorable for its harmony."

This was not wholly accurate, but near enough. The Governor had vetoed several bills, but Price's Left Wing had had much more than the required two-thirds vote of both Houses to make these bills laws over the Governor's head. This may be called harmony in a manner. Gilet now went on to say that any doubts which the Governor entertained concerning the legality of his paying any salaries could easily be settled without entering upon discussion. Discussion at such a juncture could not but tend towards informality. The President of the Council could well remember most unfortunate discussions in Missouri between the years 1856 and 1860, in some of which he had had the honor to take part *—minima pars*, gentlemen! Here he digressed elegantly upon civil dissensions, and Ballard, listening to him and marking the slow, sure progress of the hour, told himself that never before had Gilet's oratory seemed more welcome or less lengthy. A plan had come to him, the orator next announced, a way out of the present dilemma,

98

simple and regular in every aspect. Let some gentleman present now kindly draft a bill setting forth in its preamble the acts of Congress providing for the Legislature's compensation, and let this bill in conclusion provide that all members immediately receive the full amount due for their services. At noon both Houses would convene; they would push back the clock, and pass this bill before the term of their session should expire.

"Then, Gove'nuh," said Gilet, "you can amply vindicate yo'self by a veto, which, together with our votes on reconsideration of yoh objections, will be reco'ded in the journal of our proceedings, and copies transmitted to Washington within thirty days as required by law. Thus, suh, will you become absolved from all responsibility."

The orator's face, while he explained this simple and regular way out of the dilemma, beamed with acumen and statesmanship. Here they would make a law, and the Governor must obey the law!

Nothing could have been more to Ballard's mind as he calculated the fleeting minutes than this peaceful, pompous farce. "Draw your bill, gentlemen," he said. "I would not object if I could."

The Statutes of the United States were procured from among the pistols and opened at the proper page. Gascon Claiborne, upon another sheet of paper headed "Territory of Idaho, Council Chamber," set about formulating some phrases which began "Whereas," and Gratiot des Pères read aloud to him from the statutes. Ballard conversed apart with Hewley; in fact, there was much conversing aside.

"'Third March, 1863, c. 117, s. 8, v. 12, p. 811,'" dictated Des Pères.

99

"Skip the chaptuhs and sections," said Claiborne. "We only require the date."

"'Third March, 1863. The sessions of the Legislative Assemblies of the several Territories of the United States shall be limited to forty days' duration.'"

"Wise provision that," whispered Ballard. "No telling how long a poker game might last."

But Hewley could not take anything in this spirit. "Genuine business was not got through till yesterday," he said.

"'The members of each branch of the Legislature,'" read Des Pères, "' shall receive a compensation of six dollars per day during the sessions herein provided for, and they shall receive such mileage as now provided by law: *Provided*, That the President of the Council and the Speaker of the House of Representatives shall each receive a compensation of ten dollars a day.'"

At this the President of the Council waved a deprecatory hand to signify that it was a principle, not profit, for which he battled. They had completed their *Whereases*, incorporating the language of the several sections as to how the appropriation should be made, who disbursed such money, mileage, and, in short, all things pertinent to their bill, when Pete Cawthon made a suggestion.

"Ain't there anything 'bout how much the Gove'nuh gits?" he asks.

"And the Secretary?" added Wingo.

"Oh, you can leave us out," said Ballard.

"Pardon me, Gove'nuh," said Gilet. "You stated that yoh difficulty was not confined to Mr. Wingo or any individual gentleman, but was general. Does it

100

not apply to yo'self, suh? Do you not need any bill?"

"Oh no," said Ballard, laughing. "I don't need any bill."

"And why not?" said Cawthon. "You've jist ez much earned yoh money ez us fellers."

"Quite as much," said Ballard. "But we're not alike—at present."

Gilet grew very stately. "Except certain differences in political opinions, suh, I am not awah of how we differ in merit as public servants of this Territory."

"The difference is of your own making, Mr. Gilet, and no bill you could frame would cure it or destroy my responsibility. You cannot make any law contrary to a law of the United States."

"Contrary to a law of the United States? And what, suh, has the United States to say about my pay I have earned in Idaho?"

"Mr. Gilet, there has been but one government in this country since April, 1865, and as friends you and I have often agreed to differ as to how many there were before then. That government has a law compelling people like you and me to go through a formality, which I have done, and you and your friends have refused to do each time it has been suggested to you. I have raised no point until now, having my reasons, which were mainly that it would make less trouble now for the Territory of which I have been appointed Governor. I am held accountable to the Secretary of the Treasury semiannually for the manner in which the appropriation has been expended. If you will kindly hand me that book—"

Gilet, more and more stately, handed Ballard the Statutes, which he had taken from Des Pères. The

101

others were watching Ballard with gathering sullenness, as they had watched Hewley while he was winning Wingo's money, only now the sullenness was of a more decided complexion.

Ballard turned the pages. "'Second July, 1862. Every person elected or appointed to any office of honor or profit, either in the civil, military, or naval service, . . . shall, before entering upon the duties of such office, and before being entitled to any salary or other emoluments thereof, take and subscribe the following oath: I—'"

"What does this mean, suh?" said Gilet.

"It means there is no difference in our positions as to what preliminaries the law requires of us, no matter how we may vary in convictions. I as Governor have taken the oath of allegiance to the United States, and you as Councillor must do the same before you can get your pay. Look at the book."

"I decline, suh. I repudiate yoh proposition. There is a wide difference in our positions."

"What do you understand it to be, Mr. Gilet?" Ballard's temper was rising.

"If you have chosen to take an oath that did not go against yoh convictions—"

"Oh, Mr. Gilet!" said Ballard, smiling. "Look at the book." He would not risk losing his temper through further discussion. He would stick to the law as it lay open before them.

But the Northern smile sent Missouri logic to the winds. "In what are you superior to me, suh, that I cannot choose? Who are you that I and these gentlemen must take oaths befo' you?"

"Not before me. Look at the book."

"I'll look at no book, suh. Do you mean to tell

102

me you have seen me day aftuh day and meditated this treacherous attempt?"

"There is no attempt and no treachery, Mr. Gilet. You could have taken the oath long ago, like other officials. You can take it to-day—or take the consequences."

"What? You threaten me, suh? Do I understand you to threaten me? Gentlemen of the Council, it seems Idaho will be less free than Missouri unless we look to it." The President of the Council had risen in his indignant oratorical might, and his more and more restless friends glared admiration at him. "When was the time that Price's Left Wing surrendered?" asked the orator. "Nevuh! Others have, be it said to their shame. We have not toiled these thousand miles fo' that! Others have crooked the pliant hinges of the knee that thrift might follow fawning. As fo' myself, two grandfathers who fought fo' our libuhties rest in the soil of Virginia, and two uncles who fought in the Revolution sleep in the land of the Dark and Bloody Ground. With such blood in my veins I will nevuh, nevuh, nevuh submit to Northern rule and dictation. I will risk all to be with the Southern people, and if defeated I can, with a patriot of old, exclaim,

"'More true joy an exile feels
Than Cæsuh with a Senate at his heels.'

Aye, gentlemen! And we will not be defeated! Our rights are here and are ours." He stretched his arm towards the Treasurer's strong-box, and his enthusiastic audience rose at the rhetoric. "Contain yo'selves, gentlemen," said the orator. "Twelve o'clock and our bill!"

"I've said my say," said Ballard, remaining seated.

"An' what 'll ye do?" inquired Pete Cawthon from the agitated group.

"I forbid you to touch that!" shouted Ballard. He saw Wingo moving towards the box.

"Gentlemen, do not resort—" began Gilet.

But small, iron-gray Hewley snatched his pistol from the box, and sat down astraddle of it, guarding his charge. At this hostile movement the others precipitated themselves towards the table where lay their weapons, and Governor Ballard, whipping his own from his armhole, said, as he covered the table : "Go easy, gentlemen! Don't hurt our Treasurer!"

"Don't nobody hurt anybody," said Specimen Jones, opening the door.

This prudent corporal had been looking in at a window and hearing plainly for the past two minutes, and he had his men posted. Each member of the Council stopped as he stood, his pistol not quite yet attained ; Ballard restored his own to its armhole and sat in his chair; little Hewley sat on his box ; and F. Jackson Gilet towered haughtily, gazing at the intruding blue uniform of the United States.

"I'll hev to take you to the commanding officer," said Jones, briefly, to Hewley. "You and yer box."

"Oh, my stars and stripes, but that's a keen move !" rejoiced Ballard to himself. "He's arresting *us.*"

In Jones's judgment, after he had taken in the situation, this had seemed the only possible way to stop trouble without making any, and therefore, even now, bayonets were not fixed. Best not ruffle Price's Left Wing just now, if you could avoid it. For a new corporal it was well thought and done. But it was high noon, the clock not pushed back, and punctual Representatives strolling innocently towards their expected pay. There must be no time for a gathering and possible reaction. " I'll hev to clear this State-House out," Jones decided. " We're makin' an arrest," he said, aloud, "and we want a little room." The outside bystanders stood back obediently, but the Councillors delayed. Their pistols were, with Ballard's and Hewley's, of course in custody. " Here," said Jones, restoring them. "Go home now. The commanding officer's waitin' fer the prisoner. Put yer boots on, sir, and leave," he added to Pete Cawthon, who still stood in his stockings. " I don't want to hev to disperse anybody more'n what I've done."

Disconcerted Price's Left Wing now saw file out between armed soldiers the Treasurer and his strongbox; and thus guarded they were brought to Boisé Barracks, whence they did not reappear. The Governor also went to the post.

After delivering Hewley and his treasure to the commanding officer, Jones with his five troopers went to the sutler's store and took a drink at Jones's expense. Then one of them asked the corporal to have another. But Jones refused. " If a man drinks much of that," said he (and the whiskey certainly was of a livid, unlikely flavor), "he's liable to go home and steal his own pants." He walked away to his quarters, and as he went they heard him thoughtfully humming his most inveterate song, " Ye shepherds tell me have you seen my Flora pass this way."

But poisonous whiskey was not the inner reason for his moderation. He felt very much like a responsible corporal to-day, and the troopers knew it. "Jones has done himself a good turn in this fuss," they said. " He'll be changing his chevron."

That afternoon the Legislature sat in the State-

House and read to itself in the Statutes all about oaths. It is not believed that any of them sat up another night; sleeping on a problem is often much better. Next morning the commanding officer and Governor Ballard were called upon by F. Jackson Gilet and the Speaker of the House. Every one was civil and hearty as possible. Gilet pronounced the captain's whiskey "equal to any at the Southern, Saint Louey," and conversed for some time about the cold season, General Crook's remarkable astuteness in dealing with Indians, and other topics of public interest. "And concernin' yoh difficulty yesterday, Gove'nuh," said he, "I've been consulting the laws, suh, and I perceive yoh construction is entahley correct."

And so the Legislature signed that form of oath prescribed for participants in the late Rebellion, and Hewley did not have to wait for his poker money. He and Wingo played many subsequent games; for, as they all said in referring to the matter, "A little thing like that should nevuh stand between friends."

Thus was accomplished by Ballard, Paisley — and Jones—the Second Missouri Compromise, at Boisé City, Idaho, 1867—an eccentric moment in the eccentric years of our development westward, and historic also. That it has gone unrecorded until now is because of Ballard's modesty, Paisley's preference for the sword, and Jones's hatred of the pen. He was never known to write except, later, in the pages of his company roster and such unavoidable official places; for the troopers were prophetic. In not many months there was no longer a Corporal Jones, but a person widely known as Sergeant Jones of Company A; called also the "Singing Sergeant"; but still familiar to his intimate friends as "Specimen."

106

A Pilgrim on the Gila

MIDWAY from Grant to Thomas comes Paymaster's Hill, not much after Cedar Springs and not long before you sight the valley where the Gila flows. This lonely piece of road must lie three thousand miles from Washington; but in the holiday journey that I made they are near together among the adventures of mind and body that overtook me. For as I turned southward our capital was my first stopping-place, and it was here I gathered the expectations of Arizona with which I continued on my way.

Arizona was the unknown country I had chosen for my holiday, and I found them describing it in our National House of Representatives, where I had strolled for sight-seeing but stayed to listen. The Democrats were hot to make the Territory a State, while the Republicans objected that the place had about it still too much of the raw frontier. The talk and replies of each party were not long in shaking off restraint, and in the sharp exchange of satire the Republicans were reminded that they had not thought Idaho and Wyoming unripe at a season when those Territories were rumored to be Republican. Arizona might be Democratic, but neither cattle wars nor mine revolutions flourished there. Good order and prosperity prevailed. A member from Pennsylvania presently lost his temper, declaring that gigantic generalities about milk and honey and enlightenment would not avail to change his opinion. Arizona was well on to three times the size of New York—had a hundred and thirteen thousand square miles. Square miles of what? The desert of Sahara was twice as big as Arizona, and one of the largest misfortunes on the face of the earth. Arizona had sixty thousand inhabitants, not quite so many as the town of Troy. And what sort of people? He understood that cactus was Arizona's chief crop, stage-robbing her most active industry, and the Apache her leading citizen.

And then the Boy Orator of the Rio Grande took his good chance. I forgot his sallow face and black, unpleasant hair, and even his single gesture — that straining lift of one hand above the shoulder during the suspense of a sentence and that cracking it down into the other at the full stop, endless as a pile-driver. His facts wiped any trick of manner from my notice. Indians? Stage-robbers? Cactus? Yes. He would add famine, drought, impotent law, daily murder; he could add much more, but it was all told in Mr. Pumpelly's book, true as life, thirty years ago —doubtless the latest news in Pennsylvania! Had this report discouraged the gentleman from visiting Arizona? Why, he could go there to-day in a Pullman car by two great roads and eat his three meals in security. But Eastern statesmen were too often content with knowing their particular corner of our map while a continent of ignorance lay in their minds.

At this stroke applause sounded beside me, and, turning, I had my first sight of the yellow duster. The bulky man that wore it shrewdly and smilingly watched the orator, who now dwelt upon the rapid benefits of the railways, the excellent men and things they brought to Arizona, the leap into civilization that the Territory had taken. "Let Pennsylvania see those blossoming fields for herself," said he, "those boundless contiguities of shade." And a sort of cluck went off down inside my neighbor's throat, while the speaker with rising heat gave us the tonnage of plums exported from the Territory during the past fiscal year. Wool followed.

"Sock it to 'em, Limber Jim!" murmured the man in the duster, and executed a sort of step. He was plainly a personal acquaintance of the speaker's.

Figures never stick by me, nor can I quote accurately the catalogue of statistic abundance now recited in the House of Representatives; but as wheat, corn, peaches, apricots, oranges, raisins, spices, the rose and the jasmine flowered in the Boy Orator's eloquence, the genial antics of my neighbor increased until he broke into delighted mutterings, such as " He's a stud-horse," and " Put the kybosh on 'em," and many more that have escaped my memory. But the Boy Orator's peroration I am glad to remember, for his fervid convictions lifted him into the domain of metaphor and cadence; and though to be sure I made due allowance for enthusiasm, his picture of Arizona remained vivid with me, and I should have voted to make the Territory a State that very day.

"With her snow-clad summits, with the balm of her Southern vineyards, she loudly calls for a sister's rights. Not the isles of Greece, nor any cycle of Cathay, can compete with her horticultural resources, her Salt River, her Colorado, her San Pedro, her Gila,

111

her hundred irrigated valleys, each one surpassing the shaded Paradise of the Nile, where thousands of noble men and elegantly educated ladies have already located, and to which thousands more, like patient monuments, are waiting breathless to throng when the franchise is proclaimed. And if my death could buy that franchise, I would joyfully boast such martyrdom."

The orator cracked his hands together in this supreme moment, and the bulky gentleman in the duster drove an elbow against my side, whispering to me at the same time behind his hand, in a hoarse confidence: "Deserted Jericho! California only holds the record on stoves now."

" I'm afraid I do not catch your allusion," I began. But at my voice he turned sharply, and, giving me one short, ugly stare, was looking about him, evidently at some loss, when a man at his farther side pulled at his duster, and I then saw that he had all along been taking me for a younger companion he had come in with, and with whom he now went away. In the jostle we had shifted places while his eyes were upon the various speakers, and to him I seemed an eavesdropper. Both he and his friend had a curious appearance, and they looked behind them, meeting my gaze as I watched them going; and then they made to each other some laughing comment, of which I felt myself to be the inspiration. I was standing absently on the same spot, still in a mild puzzle over California and the record on stoves. Certainly I had overheard none of their secrets, if they had any; I could not even guess what might be their true opinion about admitting Arizona to our Union.

With this last memory of our Capitol and the statesmen we have collected there to govern us, I entered upon my holiday, glad that it was to be passed in such a region of enchantment. For peaches it would be too early, and with roses and jasmine I did not importantly concern myself, thinking of them only as a pleasant sight by the way. But on my gradual journey through Lexington, Bowling Green, Little Rock, and Forth Worth I dwelt upon the shade of the valleys, and the pasture hills dotted with the sheep of whose wool the Boy Orator had spoken; and I wished that our cold Northwest could have been given such a bountiful climate. Upon the final morning of railroad I looked out of the window at an earth which during the night had collapsed into a vacuum, as I had so often seen happen before upon more Northern parallels. The evenness of this huge nothing was cut by our track's interminable scar, and broken to the eye by the towns which now and again rose and littered the horizon like boxes dumped by emigrants. We were still in Texas, not distant from the Rio Grande, and I looked at the boxes drifting by, and wondered from which of them the Boy Orator had been let loose. Twice or three times upon this day of sand I saw green spots shining sudden and bright and Biblical in the wilderness. Their isolated loveliness was herald of the valley land I was nearing each hour. The wandering Mexicans, too, bright in rags and swarthy in nakedness, put me somehow in mind of the Old Testament.

In the evening I sat at whiskey with my first acquaintance, a Mr. Mowry, one of several Arizona citizens whom my military friend at San Carlos had written me to look out for on my way to visit him. My train had trundled on to the Pacific, and I sat in a

113

house once more—a saloon on the platform, with an open door through which the night air came pleasantly. This was now the long-expected Territory, and time for roses and jasmine to begin. Early in our talk I naturally spoke to Mr. Mowry of Arizona's resources and her chance of becoming a State.

"We'd have got there by now," said he, "only Luke Jenks ain't half that interested in Arizona as he is in Luke Jenks."

I reminded Mr. Mowry that I was a stranger here and unacquainted with the prominent people.

"Well, Luke's as near a hog as you kin be and wear pants. Be with you in a minute," added Mr. Mowry, and shambled from the room. This was because a shot had been fired in a house across the railroad tracks. "I run two places," he explained, returning quite soon from the house and taking up the thread of his whiskey where he had dropped it. "Two outfits. This side for toorists. Th' other pays better. I come here in 'sixty-two."

"I trust no one has been—hurt?" said I, inclining my head towards the farther side of the railroad.

"Hurt?" My question for the moment conveyed nothing to him, and he repeated the word, blinking with red eyes at me over the rim of his lifted glass. "No, nobody's hurt. I've been here a long while, and seen them as was hurt, though." Here he nodded at me depreciatingly, and I felt how short was the time that I had been here. "Th' other side pays better," he resumed, "as toorists mostly go to bed early. Six bits is about the figger you can reckon they'll spend, if you know anything." He nodded again, more solemn over his whiskey. "That kind's no help to business. I've been in this Territory from the start, and Arizona ain't

114

what it was. Them mountains are named from me."
And he pointed out of the door. "Mowry's Peak.
On the map." With this last august statement his
mind seemed to fade from the conversation, and he
struck a succession of matches along the table and various parts of his person.

"Has Mr. Jenks been in the Territory long?" I suggested, feeling the silence weigh upon me.

"Luke? He's a hog. Him the people's choice!
But the people of Arizona ain't what they was. Are
you interested in silver?"

"Yes," I answered, meaning the political question.
But before I could say what I meant he had revived
into a vigor of attitude and a wakefulness of eye of
which I had not hitherto supposed him capable.

"You come here," said he; and, catching my arm,
he took me out of the door and along the track in the
night, and round the corner of the railroad hotel into
view of more mountains that lay to the south. "You
stay here to-morrow," he pursued, swiftly, "and I'll
hitch up and drive you over there. I'll show you some
rock behind Helen's Dome that 'll beat any you've
struck in the whole course of your life. It's on the
wood reservation, and when the government abandons
the Post, as they're going to do—"

There is no need for my entering at length into his
urgence, or the plans he put to me for our becoming
partners, or for my buying him out and employing him
on a salary, or buying him out and employing some
other, or no one, according as I chose — the whole
bright array of costumes in which he presented to me
the chance of making my fortune at a stroke. I think
that from my answers he gathered presently a discour-
aging but perfectly false impression. My Eastern hat

115

and inexperienced face (I was certainly young enough
to have been his grandchild) had a little misled him ;
and although he did not in the least believe the simple
truth I told him, that I had come to Arizona on no
sort of business, but for the pleasure of seeing the
country, he now overrated my brains as greatly as he
had in the beginning despised them, quite persuaded I
was playing some game deeper than common, and either
owned already or had my eye upon other silver mines.

"Pleasure of seeing the country, ye say?" His small
wet eyes blinked as he stood on the railroad track
bareheaded, considering me from head to foot. "All
right. Did ye say ye're going to Globe?"

"No. To San Carlos to visit an army officer."

"Carlos is on the straight road to Globe," said Mr.
Mowry, vindictively. "But ye might as well drop any
idea of Globe, if ye should get one. If it's copper ye're
after, there's parties in ahead of you."

Desiring, if possible, to shift his mind from its present unfavorable turn, I asked him if Mr. Adams did
not live between here and Solomonsville, my route to
Carlos. Mr. Adams was another character of whom
my host had written me, and at my mention of his
name the face of Mr. Mowry immediately soured into
the same expression it had taken when he spoke of the
degraded Jenks.

"So you're acquainted with him ! He's got mines.
I've seen 'em. If you represent any Eastern parties,
tell 'em not to drop their dollars down old Adams's
hole in the ground. He ain't the inexperienced juniper he looks. Him and me's been acquainted these
thirty years. People claim it was Cyclone Bill held up
the Ehrenberg stage. Well, I guess I'll be seeing
how the boys are getting along."

116

With that he moved away. A loud disturbance of chairs and broken glass had set up in the house across the railroad, and I watched the proprietor shamble from me with his deliberate gait towards the establishment that paid him best. He had left me possessor of much incomplete knowledge, and I waited for him, pacing the platform ; but he did not return, and as I judged it inexpedient to follow him, I went to my bed on the tourist side of the track.

In the morning the stage went early, and as our road seemed to promise but little variety—I could see nothing but an empty plain—I was glad to find my single fellow-passenger a man inclined to talk. I did not like his mustache, which was too large for his face, nor his too careful civility and arrangement of words ; but he was genial to excess, and thoughtful of my comfort.

"I beg you will not allow my valise to incommode you," was one of his first remarks ; and I liked this consideration better than any Mr. Mowry had shown me. "I fear you will detect much initial primitiveness in our methods of transportation," he said.

This again called for gracious assurances on my part, and for a while our polite phrases balanced to corners until I was mentally winded keeping up such a pace of manners. The train had just brought him from Tucson, he told me, and would I indulge ? On this we shared and complimented each other's whiskey.

"From your flask I take it that you are a Gentile," said he, smiling.

"If you mean tenderfoot," said I, "let me confess at once that flask and owner are from the East, and brand-new in Arizona."

117

"I mean you're not a Mormon. Most strangers to me up this way are. But they carry their liquor in a plain flat bottle like this."

"Are you a—a—" Embarrassment took me as it would were I to check myself on the verge of asking a courteously disposed stranger if he had ever embezzled.

"Oh, I'm no Mormon," my new friend said, with a chuckle, and I was glad to hear him come down to reasonable English. "But Gentiles are in the minority in this valley."

"I didn't know we'd got to the valleys yet," said I, eagerly, connecting Mormons with fertility and jasmine. And I lifted the flaps of the stage, first one side and then the other, and saw the desert everywhere flat, treeless, and staring like an eye without a lid.

"This is the San Simon Valley we've been in all the time," he replied. "It goes from Mexico to the Gila, about a hundred and fifty miles."

"Like this?"

"South it's rockier. Better put the flap down."

"I don't see where people live," I said, as two smoky spouts of sand jetted from the tires and strewed over our shoes and pervaded our nostrils. "There's nothing—yes, there's one bush coming." I fastened the flaps.

"That's Seven-Mile Mesquite. They held up the stage at this point last October. But they made a mistake in the day. The money had gone down the afternoon before, and they only got about a hundred."

"I suppose it was Mormons who robbed the stage?"

"Don't talk quite so loud," the stranger said, laughing. "The driver's one of them."

"A Mormon or a robber?"

"Well, we only know he's a Mormon."

"He doesn't look twenty. Has he many wives yet?"

"Oh, they keep that thing very quiet in these days, if they do it at all. The government made things too hot altogether. The Bishop here knows what hiding for polygamy means."

"Bishop who?"

"Meakum," I thought he answered me, but was not sure in the rattle of the stage, and twice made him repeat it, putting my hand to my ear at last. "Meakum! Meakum!" he shouted.

"Yes, sir," said the driver.

"Have some whiskey?" said my friend, promptly; and when that was over and the flat bottle passed back, he explained in a lower voice, "A son of the Bishop's."

"Indeed!" I exclaimed.

"So was the young fellow who put in the mail-bags, and that yellow-headed duck in the store this morning." My companion, in the pleasure of teaching new things to a stranger, stretched his legs on the front seat, lifted my coat out of his way, and left all formality of speech and deportment. "And so's the driver you'll have to-morrow if you're going beyond Thomas, and the stock-tender at the sub-agency where you'll breakfast. He's a yellow-head too. The old man's postmaster, and owns this stage-line. One of his boys has the mail contract. The old man runs the hotel at Solomonsville and two stores at Bowie and Globe, and the store and mill at Thacher. He supplies the military posts in this district with hay and wood, and a lot of things on and off through the year. Can't write his

119

own name. Signs government contracts with his mark. He's sixty-four, and he's had eight wives. Last summer he married number nine—rest all dead, he says, and I guess that's so. He has fifty-seven recorded children, not counting the twins born last week. Any yellow-heads you'll see in the valley 'll answer to the name of Meakum as a rule, and the other type's curly black like this little driver specimen."

"How interesting there should be only two varieties of Meakum!" said I.

"Yes, it's interesting. Of course the whole fifty-seven don't class up yellow or black curly, but if you could take account of stock you'd find the big half of 'em do. Mothers don't seem to have influenced the type appreciably. His eight families, successive and simultaneous, cover a period of forty-three years, and yellow and black keeps turning up right along. Scientifically, the suppression of Mormonism is a loss to the student of heredity. Some of the children are dead. Get killed now and then, and die too—die from sickness. But you'll easily notice Meakums as you go up the valley. Old man sees all get good jobs as soon as they're old enough. Places 'em on the railroad, places 'em in town, all over the lot. Some don't stay; you couldn't expect the whole fifty-seven to be steady; but he starts 'em all fair. We have six in Tucson now, or five, maybe. Old man's a good father."

"They're not all boys?"

"Certainly not; but more than half are."

"And you say he can't write?"

"Or read, except print, and he has to spell out that."

"But, my goodness, he's postmaster!"

"What's that got to do with it? Young Meakums all read like anything. He don't do any drudgery."

"Well, you wouldn't catch me signing any contracts I couldn't read."

"Do you think you'd catch anybody reading a contract wrong to old Meakum? Oh, momma! Why, he's king round here. Fixes the county elections and the price of tomatoes. Do you suppose any Tucson jury 'll convict any of his Mormons if he says nay? No, sir! It's been tried. Why, that man ought to be in Congress."

"If he's like that I don't consider him desirable," said I.

"Yes, he is desirable," said my friend, roughly. "Smart, can't be fooled, and looks after his people's interests. I'd like to know if that don't fill the bill?"

"If he defeats justice—"

"Oh, rats!" This interruption made me regret his earlier manner, and I was sorry the polish had rubbed through so quickly and brought us to a too precipitate familiarity. "We're Western out here," he continued, "and we're practical. When we want a thing, we go after it. Bishop Meakum worked his way down here from Utah through desert and starvation, mostly afoot, for a thousand miles, and his flock to-day is about the only class in the Territory that knows what prosperity feels like, and his laws are about the only laws folks don't care to break. He's got a brain. If he weren't against Arizona's being admitted—"

"He should know better than that," said I, wishing to be friendly. "With your fruit exports and high grade of citizens you'll soon be another California."

He gave me an odd look.

"I am surprised," I proceeded, amiably, "to hear you speak of Mormons only as prosperous. They think better of you in Washington."

121

"Now, see here," said he, "I've been pleasant to you and I've enjoyed this ride. But I like plain talk."

"What's the matter?" I asked.

"And I don't care for Eastern sarcasm."

"There was no intention—"

"I don't take offence where offence is not intended. As for high-grade citizens, we don't claim to know as much as— I suppose it's New York you come from? Gold-bugs and mugwumps—"

"If you can spare the time," said I, "and kindly explain what has disturbed you in my remarks, we'll each be likely to find the rest of these forty miles more supportable."

"I guess I can stand it," said he, swallowing a drink. He folded his arms and resettled his legs; and the noisome hatefulness of his laugh filled me with regret for the wet-eyed Mowry. I would now gladly have taken any amount of Mowry in exchange for this; and it struck me afresh how uncertainly one always reckons with those who suspect their own standing.

"Till Solomonsville," said I, "let us veil our estimation of each other. Once out of this stage and the world will be large enough for both of us." I was wrong there; but presentiments do not come to me often. So I, too, drank some of my own whiskey, lighted a cigar, and observed with pleasure that my words had enraged him.

Before either of us had devised our next remark, the stage pulled up to change horses at the first and last water in forty miles. This station was kept by Mr. Adams, and I jumped out to see the man Mr. Mowry had warned me was not an inexperienced juniper. His appearance would have drawn few but missionaries to him, and I should think would have been

122

warning enough to any but an over-trustful child of six.

"Are you the geologist?" he said at once, coughing heavily; and when I told him I was simply enjoying a holiday, he looked at me sharply and spat against the corner of the stable. "There's one of them fellers expected," he continued, in a tone as if I need not attempt to deny that, and I felt his eye watching for signs of geology about me. I told him that I imagined the geologist must do an active business in Arizona.

"I don't hire 'em!" he exclaimed. "They can't tell me nothing about mineral."

"I suppose you have been here a long while, Mr. Adams?"

"There's just three living that come in ahead of—" The cough split his last word in pieces.

"Mr. Mowry was saying last night—"

"You've seen that old scamp, have you? Buy his mine behind Helen's Dome?"

My mirth at this turned him instantly confidential, and rooted his conviction that I was a geologist. "That's right!" said he, tapping my arm. "Don't you let 'em fool you. I guess you know your business. Now, if you want to look at good paying rock, thousands in sight, in sight, mind you—"

"Are you coming along with us?" called the little Meakum driver, and I turned and saw the new team was harnessed and he ready on his box, with the reins in his hands. So I was obliged to hasten from the disappointed Adams and climb back in my seat. The last I saw of him he was standing quite still in the welter of stable muck, stooping to his cough, the desert sun beating on his old body, and the desert wind

123

slowly turning the windmill above the shadeless mud hovel in which he lived alone.

"Poor old devil!" said I to my enemy, half forgetting our terms in my contemplation of Adams. "Is he a Mormon?"

My enemy's temper seemed a little improved. "He's tried most everything except jail," he answered, his voice still harsh. "You needn't invest your sentiment there. He used to hang out at Twenty Mile in Old Camp Grant days, and he'd slit your throat for fifty cents."

But my sentiment was invested somehow. The years of the old-timers were ending so gray. Their heyday, and carousals, and happy-go-luckiness all gone, and in the remaining hours—what? Empty youth is such a grand easy thing, and empty age so grim!

"Has Mowry tried everything, too?" I asked.

"Including jail," said my companion ; and gave me many entertaining incidents of Mowry's career with an ill-smelling saloon cleverness that put him once more into favorable humor with me, while I retained my opinion of him. "And that uneducated sot," he concluded, "that hobo with his record of cattle-stealing and claim-jumping, and his acquittal from jail through railroad influence, actually undertook to run against me last elections. My name is Jenks ; Luke Jenks, Territorial Delegate from Arizona." He handed me his card.

"I'm just from Washington," said I.

"Well, I've not been there this session. Important law business has detained me here. Yes, they backed Mowry in that election. The old spittoon had quite a following, but he hadn't the cash. That gives you some idea of the low standards I have to combat.

But I hadn't to spend much. This Territory's so poor they come cheap. Seventy-five cents a head for all the votes I wanted in Bisbee, Nogales, and Yuma; and up here the Bishop was my good friend. Holding office booms my business some, and that's why I took it, of course. But I've had low standards to fight."

The Territorial Delegate now talked freely of Arizona's frontier life. "It's all dead," he said, forgetting in his fluency what he had told me about Seven-Mile Mesquite and last October. "We have a community as high toned as any in the land. Our monumental activity—" And here he went off like a cuckoo clock, or the Boy Orator, reciting the glories of Phœnix and Salt River, and the future of silver, in that special dialect of platitudes which is spoken by our more talkative statesmen, and is not quite Latin, quite grammar, or quite falsehood. "We're not all Mowrys and Adamses," said he, landing from his flight.

"In a population of fifty-nine thousand," said I, heartily, "a stranger is bound to meet decent people if he keeps on."

Again he misinterpreted me, but this time the other way, bowing like one who acknowledges a compliment; and we came to Solomonsville in such peace that he would have been astonished at my private thoughts. For I had met no undisguised vagabond nor out-and-out tramp whom I did not prefer to Luke Jenks, vote-buyer and politician. With his catch-penny plausibility, his thin-spread good-fellowship, and his New York clothes, he mistook himself for a respectable man, and I was glad to be done with him.

I could have reached Thomas that evening, but after our noon dinner let the stage go on, and delayed a night for the sake of seeing the Bishop hold service

125

next day, which was Sunday, some few miles down the valley. I was curious to learn the Mormon ritual and what might be the doctrines that such a man as the Bishop would expound. It dashed me a little to find this would cost me forty-eight hours of Solomonsville, no Sunday stage running. But one friendly English-speaking family—the town was chiefly Mexican—made some of my hours pleasant, and others I spent in walking. Though I went early to bed I slept so late that the ritual was well advanced when I reached the Mormon gathering. From where I was obliged to stand I could only hear the preacher, already in the middle of his discourse.

"Don't empty your swill in the door-yard, but feed it to your hogs," he was saying; and any one who knows how plainly a man is revealed in his voice could have felt instantly, as I did, that here was undoubtedly a leader of men. "Rotten meat, rotten corn, spoiled milk, the truck that thoughtless folks throw away, should be used. Their usefulness has not ceased because they're rotten. That's the error of the ignorant, who know not that nothing is meant to be wasted in this world. The ignorant stay poor because they break the law of the Lord. Waste not, want not. The children of the Gentiles play in the door-yard and grow sickly and die. The mother working in the house has a pale face and poison in her blood. She cannot be a strong wife. She cannot bear strong sons to the man. He stays healthy because he toils in the field. He does not breathe the tainted air rising from the swill in the door-yard. Swill is bad for us, but it is good for swine. Waste it by the threshold it becomes deadly, and a curse falls upon the house. The mother and children are sick because

126

she has broken a law of the Lord. Do not let me see this sin when I come among you in the valley. Fifty yards behind each house, with clean air between, let me see the well-fed swine receiving each day, as was intended, the garbage left by man. And let me see flowers in the door-yard, and stout, blooming children. We will sing the twenty-ninth hymn."

The scales had many hours ago dropped from my eyes, and I saw Arizona clear, and felt no repining for roses and jasmine. They had been a politician's way of foisting one more silver State upon our Senate, and I willingly renounced them for the real thing I was getting; for my holiday already far outspangled the motliest dream that ever visited me, and I settled down to it as we settle down in our theatre chairs, well pleased with the flying pantomime. And when, after the hymn and a blessing—the hymn was poor stuff about wanting to be a Mormon and with the Mormons stand—I saw the Bishop get into a wagon, put on a yellow duster, and drive quickly away, no surprise struck me at all. I merely said to myself: Certainly. How dull not to have foreseen that! And I knew that we should speak together soon, and he would tell me why California only held the record on stoves.

But oh, my friends, what a country we live in, and what an age, that the same stars and stripes should simultaneously wave over this and over Delmonico's! This too I kept thinking as I killed more hours in walking the neighborhood of Solomonsville, an object of more false hope to natives whom I did not then observe. I avoided Jenks, who had business clients in the town. I went among the ditches and the fields thus turned green by the channelled Gila; and though it was scarce a paradise surpassing the Nile, it was grassy and full of sweet smells until after a few miles each way, when the desert suddenly met the pleasant verdure full in the face and corroded it to death like vitriol.   The sermon came back to me as I passed the little Mormon homes, and the bishop rose and rose in my esteem, though not as one of the children of light. That sagacious patriarch told his flock the things of week - day wisdom down to their level, the cleanly things next to godliness, to keep them from the million squalors that stain our Gentile poor; and if he did not sound much like the Gospel, he and Deuteronomy were alike as two peas.   With him and Moses thus in my thoughts, I came back after sunset, and was gratified to be late for supper.   Jenks had left the dining - room, and I ate in my own company, which had become lively and full of intelligent impressions. These I sat recording later in my journal, when a hesitating knock came at my bedroom, and two young men in cowboy costume entered like shy children, endeavoring to step without creaking.

"Meakums!" my delighted mind exclaimed, inwardly; but the yellow one introduced the black curly one as Mr. Follet, who, in turn, made his friend Mr. Cunningham known to me, and at my cordial suggestion they sat down with increasing awkwardness, first leaving their hats outside the door.

"We seen you walking around," said one.

"Lookin' the country over," said the other.

"Fine weather for travelling," said the first.

"Dusty though," said the second.

Perceiving them to need my help in coming to their point, I said, "And now about your silver mine."

"You've called the turn on us!" exclaimed yellow,

and black curly slapped his knee. Both of them sat looking at me, laughing enthusiastically, and I gathered they had been having whiskey this Sunday night. I confess that I offered them some more, and when they realized my mildness they told me with length and confidence about the claims they had staked out on Mount Turnbull. " And there's lots of lead, too," said yellow.

" I do not smelt," said I, " or deal in any way with ore. I have come here without the intention of buying anything."

" You ain't the paymaster?" burst out black curly, wrinkling his forehead like a pleasant dog.

Yellow touched his foot.

" Course he ain't!" said curly, with a swerve of his eye. " He ain't due. What a while it always is waitin'!"

Now the paymaster was nothing to me, nor whom he paid. For all I knew, my visitors were on his roll; and why yellow should shy at the mention of him and closely watch his tipsy mate I did not try to guess. Like every one I had met so far in Arizona, these two evidently doubted I was here for my pleasure merely; but it was with entire good-humor that they remarked a man had the right to mind his own business; and so, with a little more whiskey, we made a friendly parting. They recommended me to travel with a pistol in this country, and I explained that I should do myself more harm than good with a weapon that any one handled more rapidly than I, with my inexperience.

" Good-night, Mr. Meakum," I said.

" Follet," corrected black curly.

" Cunningham," said yellow, and they picked up their hats in the hall and withdrew.

I think now those were their names—the time was coming when I should hear them take oath on it—yet I do not know. I heard many curious oaths taken.

I was glad to see black curly in the stage next day, not alone for his company, but to give him a right notion of what ready money I had about me. Thinking him over, and his absence of visible means of support, and his interest in me, I took opportunity to mention, quite by the way, that five or six dollars was all that I ever carried on my person, the rest being in New York drafts, worthless in any hands but mine. And I looked at the time once or twice for him to perceive the cheapness of my nickel watch. That the Bishop was not his father I had indirect evidence when we stopped at Thacher to change horses and drop a mail - sack, and the Mormon divine suddenly lifted the flap and inspected us. He nodded to me and gave Follet a message.

"Tell your brother" (wouldn't a father have said Tom or Dick?) "that I've given him chances enough and he don't take em. He don't feed my horses, and my passengers complain he don't feed them—though that's not so serious!" said he to me, with a jovial wink. "But I won't have my stock starved. You'll skip the station and go through to Thomas with this pair," he added to the driver in his voice of lusty command. "You'll get supper at Thomas. Everything's moved on there from to-day. That's the rule now." Then he returned to black curly, who, like the driver, had remained cowed and respectful throughout the short harangue. "Your brother could have treated me square and made money by that station. Tell him that, and to see me by Thursday. If he's thinking of peddling vegetables this season I'll let him sell to

Fort Bowie. Safford takes Carlos, and I won't have two compete in the same market, or we'll be sinking low as Eastern prices," said he to me, with another wink. "Drive on now. You're late."

He shut the flap, and we were off quickly—too quickly. In the next few moments I could feel that something all wrong went on; there was a jingle and snapping of harness, and such a voice from the Bishop behind us that I looked out to see him. We had stopped, and he was running after us at a wonderful pace for a man of sixty-four.

"If you don't drive better than that," said the grizzled athlete, arriving cool and competent, "you'll saw wood for another year. Look how you've got them trembling."

It was a young pair, and they stood and steamed while the broken gear was mended.

"What did California hold the record in before the Boy Orator broke it?" said I, getting out.

He shot at me the same sinister look I had seen in the Capitol, the look he must always wear, I suppose, when taken aback. Then he laughed broadly and heartily, a strong pleasant laugh that nearly made me like him. "So you're that fellow! Ho, ho! Away down here now. Oh, ho, ho! What's your business?"

"You wouldn't believe if I told you," said I, to his sudden sharp question.

"Me? Why, I believe everything I'm told. What's your name?"

"Will you believe I haven't come to buy anybody's silver mine?"

"Silver! I don't keep it. Unloaded ten years ago before the rabbit died."

"Then you're the first anti-silver man I've met."

131

"I'm anti anything I can't sell, young man. Here's all there is to silver: Once upon a time it was hard to get, and we had to have it. Now it's easy. When it gets as common as dirt it'll be as cheap as dirt. Same as watermelons when it's a big crop. D'you follow me? That's silver for you, and I don't want it. So you've come away down here. Well, well! What did you say your name was?"

I told him.

"Politician?"

"God forbid!"

"Oh, ho, ho! Well, yes. I took a look at those buzzards there in Washington. Our Senate and Representatives. They were screeching a heap. All about ratios. You'll be sawing wood yet!" he shouted to the driver, and strode up to help him back a horse. "Now ratio is a good-sounding word too, and I guess that's why they chew on it so constant. Better line of language that they get at home. I'll tell you about Congress. Here's all there is to it: You can divide them birds in two lots. Those who know better and those who don't. D'you follow me?"

"And which kind is the Boy Orator?"

"Limber Jim? Oh, he knows better. I know Jim. You see, we used to have a saying in Salt Lake that California had the smallest stoves and the biggest liars in the world. Now Jim—well, there's an old saying busted. But you'll see Arizona 'll go back on the Democrats. If they put wool on the free list she'll stay Republican, and they won't want her admitted, which suits me first-rate. My people here are better off as they stand."

"But your friend Mr. Jenks favors admission!" I exclaimed.

132

"Luke? He's been talking to you, has he? Well now, Luke. Here's all there is to him: Natural gas. That's why I support him, you see. If we sent a real smart man to Washington he might get us made a State. Ho, ho! But Luke stays here most of the time, and he's no good anyway. Oh, ho, ho! So you're buying no mines this season?"

Once more I found myself narrating the insignificance of my visit to Arizona—the Bishop must have been a hard inquisitor for even the deeply skilful to elude—and for the first time my word was believed. He quickly took my measure, saw that I had nothing to hide, and after telling me I could find good hunting and scenery in the mountains north, paid me no further attention, but masterfully laid some final commands on the intimidated driver. Then I bade goodbye to the Bishop, and watched that old locomotive moving vigorously back along the road to his manifold business.

The driver was ill pleased to go hungry for his supper until Thomas, but he did not dare complain much over the new rule, even to black curly and me. This and one other thing impressed me. Some miles farther on we had passed out of the dust for a while, and rolled up the flaps.

"She's waiting for you," said the driver to black curly, and that many-sided youth instantly dived to the bottom of the stage, his boots and pistol among my legs.

"Throw your coat over me," he urged.

I concealed him with that and a mail-sack, and stretched my head out to see what lioness stood in his path. But it was only a homelike little cabin, and at the door a woman, comely and mature, eying the stage expectantly. Possibly wife, I thought, more likely mother, and I asked, " Is Mrs. Follet strict ?" choosing a name to fit either.

The driver choked and chirruped, but no sound came from under the mail-sack until we had passed the good-day to the momentous female, whose response was harsh with displeasure as she wheeled into her door. A sulky voice then said, " Tell me when she's gone, Bill." But we were a safe two hundred yards on the road before he would lift his head, and his spirits were darkened during the remainder of the journey.

" Come and live East," said I, inviting him to some whiskey at the same time. " Back there they don't begin sitting up for you so early in the evening."

This did not enliven him, although upon our driver it seemed to bring another fit as much beyond the proportion of my joke as his first had been. " She tires a man's spirit," said black curly, and with this rueful utterance he abandoned the subject; so that when we reached Thomas in the dim night my curiosity was strong, and I paid little heed to this new place where I had come or to my supper. Black curly had taken himself off, and the driver sat at the table with me, still occasionally snickering in his plate. He would explain nothing that I asked him until the gaunt woman who waited on us left us for the kitchen, when he said, with a nervous, hasty relish, " The Widow Sproud is slick," and departed.

Consoled by no better clew than this I went to bed in a down-stairs room, and in my strange rising next day I did not see the driver again. Callings in the air awaked me, and a wandering sound of wheels. The gaunt woman stood with a lamp in my room say-

134

ing the stage was ready, and disappeared. I sprang
up blindly, and again the callings passed in the blackness outside—long cries, inarticulate to me. Wheels
heavily rolled to my door, and a whip was struck
against it, and there loomed the stage, and I made
out the calling. It was the three drivers, about to
separate before the dawn on their three diverging
ways, and they were wailing their departure through
the town that travellers might hear, in whatever place
they lay sleeping. "Boo-wie! All aboa-rd!" came
from somewhere, dreary and wavering, met at farther distance by the floating antiphonal, "Aboa-rd,
aboa-rd for Grant!" and in the chill black air my
driver lifted his portion of the strain, chanting, "Carlos! Car-los!" One last time he circled in the nearer darkness with his stage to let me dress. Mostly
unbuttoned, and with not even a half minute to
splash cold water in my eyes, I clambered solitary
into the vehicle and sat among the leather mail-bags,
some boxes, and a sack of grain, having four hours
yet till breakfast for my contemplation. I heard the
faint reveille at Camp Thomas, but to me it was a call
for more bed, and I pushed and pulled the grain-sack
until I was able to distribute myself and in a manner
doze, shivering in my overcoat. Not the rising of the
sun upon this blight of sand, nor the appearance of a
cattle herd, and both black curly and yellow driving
it among its dust clouds, warmed my frozen attention
as I lay in a sort of spell. I saw with apathy the
mountains, extraordinary in the crystal prism of the
air, and soon after the strangest scene I have ever
looked on by the light of day. For as we went along
the driver would give a cry, and when an answering
cry came from the thorn-bush we stopped, and a naked

135

Indian would appear, running, to receive a little parcel of salt or sugar or tobacco he had yesterday given the driver some humble coin to buy for him in Thomas. With changeless pagan eyes staring a moment at me on my sack of grain, and a grunt when his purchase was set in his hands, each black-haired desert figure turned away, the bare feet moving silent, and the copper body, stark naked except the breech-clout, receding to dimness in the thorn-bush. But I lay incurious at this new vision of what our wide continent holds in fee under the single title United States, until breakfast came. This helped me, and I livened somewhat at finding the driver and the breakfast man were both genuine Meakums, as Jenks had told me they would be.

It surprised me to discover now that I was looked for along the Gila, and my name approximately known, and when I asked if my friend Captain Stirling had spoken of my coming, it was evidently not he, but the news was in the air. This was a prominence I had never attained in any previous part of the world, and I said to the driver that I supposed my having no business made me a curiosity. That might have something to do with it, he answered (he seemed to have a literal mind), but some had thought I was the paymaster.

"Folks up here," he explained, "are liable to know who's coming."

"If I lived here," said I, "I should be anxious for the paymaster to come early and often."

"Well, it does the country good. The soldiers spend it all right here, and us civilians profit some by it."

Having got him into conversation, I began to introduce the subject of black curly, hoping to lead up to the Widow Sproud; but before I had compassed this we reached San Carlos, where a blow awaited me. Stirling, my host, had been detailed on a scout this morning! I was stranded here, a stranger, where I had come thousands of miles to see an old friend. His regret and messages to make myself at home, and the quartermaster's hearty will to help me to do so could not cure my blankness. He might be absent two weeks or more. I looked round at Carlos and its staring sand. Then I resolved to go at once to my other friends now stationed at Fort Grant. For I had begun to feel myself at an immense distance from any who would care what happened to me for good or ill, and I longed to see some face I had known before. So in gloom I retraced some unattractive steps. This same afternoon I staged back along the sordid, incompetent Gila River, and to kill time pushed my Sproud inquiry, at length with success. To check the inevitably slipshod morals of a frontier commonwealth, Arizona has a statute that in reality only sets in writing a presumption of the common law, the ancient presumption of marriage, which is that when a man and woman go to house-keeping for a certain length of time, they shall be deemed legally married. In Arizona this period is set at twelve months, and ten had run against Mrs. Sproud and young Follet. He was showing signs of leaving her. The driver did not think her much entitled to sympathy, and certainly she showed later that she could devise revenge. As I thought over these things we came again to the cattle herd, where my reappearance astonished yellow and black curly. Nor did the variance between my movements and my reported plans

137

seem wholly explained to them by Stirling's absence, and at the station where I had breakfasted I saw them question the driver about me. This interest in my affairs heightened my desire to reach Fort Grant ; and when next day I came to it after another waking to the chanted antiphonals and another faint reveille from Camp Thomas in the waning dark, extreme comfort spread through me. I sat in the club with the officers, and they taught me a new game of cards called Solo, and filled my glass. Here were lieutenants, captains, a major, and a colonel, American citizens with a love of their country and a standard of honor ; here floated our bright flag serene against the lofty blue, and the mellow horns sounded at guard-mounting, bringing moisture to the eyes. The day was punctuated with the bright trumpet, people went and came in the simple dignity of duty, and once again I talked with good men and women. God bless our soldier people ! I said it often.

They somewhat derided my uneasiness in the Gila Valley, and found my surmisings sensational. Yet still they agreed much ready money was an unwise thing on a stage journey, although their profession (I suppose) led them to take being " held up" less seriously than I with my peaceful traditions of elevators and the down-town lunch. In the wide Sulphur Springs valley where I rode at large, but never so long or so far that Fort Grant lay not in sight across that miracle of air, it displeased me to come one morning upon yellow and black curly jogging along beneath the government telegraph line.

"You cover a wide range," said I.

"Cowboys have to," they answered. "So you've not quit us yet?"

"I'm thinking of taking a hunt and fish towards Fort Apache."

"We're your men, then. You'll find us at Thomas any time. We're gathering stock up these draws, but that 'll be through this week."

They spurred their horses and vanished among the steep little hills that run up to Mount Graham. But indeed they should be no men of mine! Stirling had written me his scout was ended, and San Carlos worth a longer visit than I had made there, promising me an escort should I desire to camp in the mountains. An escort it should be, and no yellow or black curly, over-curious about my private matters! This fell in excellently with the coming paymaster's movements. Major Pidcock was even now on his way to Fort Grant from Fort Bowie; and when he went to Thomas and Carlos I would go, too, in his ambulance; and I sighed with pleasure at escaping that stage again.

Major Pidcock arrived in a yellow duster, but in other respects differed from the Bishop, though in his body a bulky man. We were introduced to each other at the club.

"I am glad, sir, to meet you at last," I said to him. "The whole Gila Valley has been taking me for you."

"Oh—ah!" said Pidcock, vaguely, and pulling at some fat papers in his coat; "indeed. I understand that is a very ignorant population. Colonel Vincent, a word with you. The Department Commander requests me—" And here he went off into some official talk with the Colonel.

I turned among the other officers, who were standing by an open locker having whiskey, and Major Evlie put his hand on my shoulder. "He doesn't

139

mean anything," he whispered, while the rest looked knowingly at me. Presently the Colonel explained to Pidcock that he would have me to keep him company to Carlos.

"Oh—ah, Colonel. Of course we don't take civilians not employed by the government, as a rule. But exceptions—ah—can be made," he said to me. "I will ask you to be ready immediately after breakfast to-morrow." And with that he bowed to us all and sailed forth across the parade-ground.

The Colonel's face was red. and he swore in his quiet voice; but the lips of the lieutenants by the open locker quivered fitfully in the silence.

"Don't mind Pidcock," Evlie remarked. "He's a paymaster." And at this the line officers became disorderly, and two lieutenants danced together; so that, without catching Evlie's evidently military joke, I felt pacified.

"And I've got to have him to dinner," sighed the Colonel, and wandered away.

"You'll get on with him, man—you'll get on with him in the ambulance," said my friend Paisley. "Flatter him, man. Just ask him about his great strategic stroke at Cayuse Station that got him his promotion to the pay department."

Well, we made our start after breakfast, Major Pidcock and I, and another passenger too, who sat with the driver—a black cook going to the commanding officer's at Thomas. She was an old plantation mammy, with a kind but bewildered face, and I am sorry that the noise of our driving lost me much of her conversation; for whenever we slowed, and once when I walked up a hill, I found her remarks to be steeped in a flighty charm.

140

"Fo' Lawd's sake!" said she. "W'at's dat?" And when the driver told her that it was a jack-rabbit, "You go 'long!" she cried, outraged. "I'se seed rabbits earlier 'n de mawnin' dan yo'self." She watched the animal with all her might, muttering, "Law, see him squot," and "Hole on, hole on!" and "Yasser, he done gone fo' sho. My grashus, you lemme have a scatter shoot-gun an' a spike-tail smell dog, an' I'll git one of dey narrah-gauge mules."

"I shall not notice it," said Major Pidcock to me, with dignity. "But they should have sent such a creature by the stage. It's unsuitable, wholly."

"Unquestionably," said I, straining to catch the old lady's song on the box:

> "'Don't you fo'git I's a-comin' behind you—
> Lam slam de lunch ham.'"

"This is insufferable," said Pidcock. "I shall put her off at Cedar Springs."

I suppose the drive was long to him, but to me it was not. Noon and Cedar Springs prematurely ended the first half of this day most memorable in the whole medley of my excursion, and we got down to dine. Two travellers bound for Thomas by our same road were just setting out, but they firmly declined to transport our cook, and Pidcock moodily saw them depart in their wagon, leaving him burdened still; for this was the day the stage made its down trip from Thomas. Never before had I seen water paid for. When the Major, with windy importance, came to settle his bill, our dozen or fourteen escort horses and mules made an item, the price of watering two head being two bits, quite separate from the

141

feed; and I learned that water was thus precious over most of the Territory.

Our cook remounted the box in high feather, and began at once to comment upon Arizona. "Dere ain't no winter, nor no spring, nor no rain de hole year roun'. My! what a country fo' to gib de chick-'ns courage! Dey hens must jus' sit an' lay an' lay. But de po' ducks done have a mean time.

"'O—Lawd!
Sinner is in my way, Daniel.'"

"I would not permit a cook like that inside my house," said Major Pidcock.

"She may not be dangerous," I suggested.

"Land! is dey folks gwineter shoot me?" Naturally I looked, and so did the Major; but it was two of our own mounted escort that she saw out to the right of us among the hills. "Tell dem nigger jockeys I got no money. Why do dey triflin' chillun ride in de kerridge?" She did not mean ourselves, but the men with their carbines in the escort wagon in front of us. I looked out at them, and their mouths were wide open for joy at her. It was not a stately prog-ress for twenty-eight thousand dollars in gold and a paymaster to be making. Major Pidcock unbottoned his duster and reclined to sleep, and presently I also felt the after-dinner sloth shutting my eyes pleasantly to this black road.

"Heave it, chillun! can't you heave?" I heard our cook say, and felt us stop.

"What's that?" I asked, drowsily.

"Seems to be a rock fallen down," the Major an-swered. "Start it, men; roll it!"

I roused myself. We were between rocks and banks

142

on the brow of a hill, down which the narrow road descended with a slight turn. I could see the escort wagon halted ahead of us, and beyond it the men stooping at a large stone, around which there was no possible room to drive. This stone had fallen, I reflected, since those travellers for Thomas—

There was a shot, and a mule rolled over.

I shall never forget that. It was like the theatre for one paralyzed second! The black soldiers, the mule, the hill, all a clear picture seen through an opera-glass, stock-still, and nothing to do with me— for a congealed second. And, dear me, what a time we had then!

Crackings volleyed around us, puffs of smoke jetted blue from rock ramparts which I had looked at and thought natural—or, rather, not thought of at all— earth and gravel spattered up from the ground, the bawling negress spilled off her box and ran in spirals, screaming, "Oh, bless my soul, bless my soul!" and I saw a yellow duster flap out of the ambulance. "Lawd grashus, he's a-leavin' us!" screeched the cook, and she changed her spirals for a bee-line after him. I should never have run but for this example, for I have not naturally the presence of mind, and in other accidents through which I have passed there has never been promptness about me; the reasoning and all has come when it was over, unless it went on pretty long, when I have been sometimes able to leap to a conclusion. But yes, I ran now, straight under a screen of rocks, over the top of which rose the heads of yellow and black curly. The sight of them sent rushing over me the first agreeable sensation I had felt—shapeless rage—and I found myself shouting at them, "Scoundrels! scoundrels!" while shooting continued briskly around me. I think my performance would have sincerely entertained them could they have spared the time for it; and as it was, they were regarding me with obvious benevolence, when Mr. Adams looked evilly at me across the stones, and black curly seized the old devil's rifle in time to do me a good turn. Mr. Adams's bullet struck short of me ten feet, throwing the earth in my face. Since then I have felt no sympathy for that tobacco-running pioneer. He listened, coughing, to what black curly said as he pointed to me, and I see now that I have never done a wiser thing than to go unarmed in that country. Curly was telling Mr. Adams that I was harmless. Indeed, that was true! In the bottom of this cup, target for a circled rim of rifles, separated from the widely scattered Major and his men, aware of nothing in particular, and seeing nothing in particular but smoke and rocks and faces peering everywhere, I walked to a stone and sat upon it, hypnotized again into a spectator. From this undisturbed vantage I saw shape itself the theft of the gold—the first theft, that is; for it befell me later to witness a ceremony by which these eagles of Uncle Sam again changed hands in a manner that stealing is as good a name for as any.

They had got two mules killed, so that there could be no driving away in a hurry, and I saw that killing men was not a part of their war, unless required as a means to their end. Major Pidcock had spared them this necessity; I could see him nowhere; and with him to imitate I need not pause to account for the members of our dismounted escort. Two soldiers, indeed, lay on the ground, the sergeant and another, who had evidently fired a few resisting shots;

144

but let me say at once that these poor fellows recovered, and I saw them often again through this adventure that bound us together, else I could not find so much hilarity in my retrospect. Escort wagon and ambulance stood empty and foolish on the road, and there lay the ingenious stone all by itself, and the carbines all by themselves foolish in the wagon, where the innocent soldiers had left them on getting out to move the stone. Smoke loitered thin and blue over this now exceedingly quiet scene, and I smelt it where I sat. How secure the robbers had felt themselves, and how reckless of identification! Mid-day, a public road within hearing of a ranch, an escort of a dozen regulars, no masks, and the stroke perpetrated at the top of a descent, contrary to all laws of road agency. They swarmed into sight from their ramparts. I cannot tell what number, but several I had never seen before and never saw again; and Mr. Adams and yellow and black curly looked so natural that I wondered if Jenks and the Bishop would come climbing down too. But no more old friends turned up that day. Some went to the ambulance swift and silent, while others most needlessly stood guard. Nothing was in sight but my seated inoffensive form, and the only sound was, somewhere among the rocks, the voice of the incessant negress speeding through her prayers. I saw them at the ambulance, surrounding, passing, lifting, stepping in and out, ferreting, then moving slowly up with their booty round the hill's brow. Then silence; then hoofs; then silence again, except the outpouring negress, scriptural, melodious, symbolic:

"'Oh—Lawd!
Sinner is in my way, Daniel.'"

145

All this while I sat on the stone. "They have done us brown," I said aloud, and hearing my voice waked me from whatever state I had been in. My senses bounded, and I ran to the hurt soldiers. One was very sick. I should not have known what to do for them, but people began to arrive, brought from several quarters by the fusillade — two in a wagon from Cedar Springs, two or three on horses from the herds they were with in the hills, and a very old man from somewhere, who offered no assistance to any one, but immediately seated himself and began explaining what we all should have done. The negress came out of her rocks, exclamatory with pity over the wounded, and, I am bound to say, of more help to them than any of us, kind and motherly in the midst of her ceaseless discourse. Next arrived Major Pidcock in his duster, and took charge of everything.

"Let yer men quit the'r guns, did ye, general?" piped the very old man. "Escort oughtn't never to quit the'r guns. I seen that at Molino del Rey. And ye should have knowed that there stone didn't crawl out in the road like a turtus to git the sunshine."

"Where were you?" thundered the Major to the mounted escort, who now appeared, half an hour after the event, from our flanks, which they had been protecting at an immense distance. "Don't you know your duty's to be on hand when you hear firing?"

"Law, honey!" said the cook, with a guffaw, "lemme git my han's over my mouf."

"See them walls they fooled yer with!" continued the old man, pointing with his stick. "I could have told yer them wasn't natural. Them doesn't show like country rock;" by which I found that he meant their faces were new-exposed and not weather-beaten.

146

"No doubt you could have saved us, my friend," said the Major, puffing blandly.

But one cannot readily impress ninety summers. "Yes, I could have told yer that," assented the sage, with senile complacence. "My wife could have told yer that. Any smart girl could have told yer that."

"I shall send a despatch for re-enforcements," announced Pidcock. "Tap the telegraph wire," he ordered.

"I have to repawt to the Major," said a soldier, saluting, "dat de line is cut."

At this I was taken with indecent laughter, and turned away, while ninety summers observed, "Of course them boys would cut the wire if they knew their business."

Swearing capably, the Major now accounted clearly to us for the whole occurrence, striding up and down, while we lifted the hurt men into the ranch wagon, and arranged for their care at Cedar Springs. The escort wagon hurried on to Thomas for a doctor. The ambulance was, of course, crippled of half its team, and the dead mules were cleared from their harness and got to the road-side. Having satisfactorily delivered himself of his explanation, the Major now organized a party for following the trail of the robbers, to learn into what region they had betaken themselves. Incredible as it may seem, after my late unenterprising conduct, I asked one of the riders to lend me his horse, which he did, remarking that he should not need it for an hour, and that he was willing to risk my staying absent longer than that.

So we rode away. The trail was clear, and we had but little trouble to follow it. It took us off to the right through a mounded labyrinth of hillocks, puny and gray like ash-heaps, where we rose and fell in the trough of the sullen landscape. I told Pidcock of my certainty about three of the robbers, but he seemed to care nothing for this, and was something less than civil at what he called my suggestions.

"When I have ascertained their route," he said, "it will be time enough to talk of their identity."

In this way we went for a mile or so, the trail leading us onward, frank and straight, to the top of a somewhat higher hill, where it suddenly expired off the earth. No breath vanishes cleaner from glass, and it brought us to a dead halt. We retraced the tracks to make sure we had not lost them before, but there was no mistake, and again we halted dead at the vanishing-point. Here were signs that something out of the common had happened. Men's feet and horseshoe prints, aimless and superimposed, marked a trodden frame of ground, inside which was nothing, and beyond which nothing lay but those faint tracks of wandering cattle and horses that scatter everywhere in this country. Not one defined series, not even a single shod horse, had gone over this hill, and we spent some minutes vainly scouring in circles wider and wider. Often I returned to stare at the trodden, imperturbable frame of ground, and caught myself inspecting first the upper air, and next the earth, and speculating if the hill were hollow; and mystery began to film over the hitherto sharp figures of black curly and yellow, while the lonely country around grew so unpleasant to my nerves that I was glad when Pidcock decided that he must give up for to-day. We found the little group of people beginning to disperse at the ambulance.

"Fooled yer ag'in, did they?" said the old man.

148

"Played the blanket trick on yer, I expect. Guess yer gold's got pretty far by now." With this parting, and propped upon his stick, he went as he had come. Not even at any time of his youth, I think, could he have been companionable, and old age had certainly filled him with the impartial malevolence of the devil. I rejoice to say that he presided at none of our further misadventures.

Short twenty-eight thousand dollars and two mules, we set out anew, the Major, the cook, and I, along the Thomas road, with the sun drawing closer down upon the long steel saw that the peaks to our westward made. The site of my shock lay behind me—I knew now well enough that it had been a shock, and that for a long while to come I should be able to feel the earth spatter from Mr. Adams's bullet against my ear and sleeve whenever I might choose to conjure that moment up again—and the present comfort in feeling my distance from that stone in the road increase continually put me in more cheerful spirits. With the quick rolling of the wheels many subjects for talk came into my mind, and had I been seated on the box beside the cook we should have found much in common. Ever since her real tenderness to those wounded men I had wished to ask the poor old creature how she came in this weary country, so far from the pleasant fields of cotton and home. Her hair was gray, and she had seen much, else she had never been so kind and skilful at bandaging. And I am quite sure that somewhere in the chambers of her incoherent mind and simple heart abided the sweet ancient fear of God and love of her fellow-men—virtues I had met but little in Arizona.

"De hole family, scusin' two," she was saying, "dey

149

bust loose and tuck to de woods." And then she moralized upon the two who stayed behind and were shot. "But de Gennul he 'low dat wuz mighty pore reasonin'."

I should have been glad to exchange views with her, for Major Pidcock was dull company. This prudent officer was not growing distant from his disaster, and as night began to come, and we neared Thomas, I suppose the thought that our ambulance was driving him perhaps to a court-martial was enough to submerge the man in gloom. To me and my news about the robbers he was a little more considerate, although he still made nothing of the fact that some of them lived in the Gila Valley, and were of the patriarchal tribe of Meakum.

"Scoundrels like that," he muttered, lugubriously, "know every trail in the country, and belong nowhere. Mexico is not a long ride from here. They can get a steamer at Guaymas and take their choice of ports down to Valparaiso. Yes, they'll probably spend that money in South America. Oh, confound that woman!"

For the now entirely cheerful negress was singing:

"'Dar's de gal, dar's my Susanna.
How by gum you know?
Know her by de red bandanna,
An' de shoestring hangin' on de flo'—
Dad blam her!—
An' de shoestring hangin'—

Goodness grashus! what *you* gwineter do?"

At this sudden cry and the stopping of the ambulance I thought more people were come for our gold, and my spirit resigned itself. Sit still was all I should do now, and look for the bright day when I should leave Arizona forever. But it was only Mrs. Sproud. I had clean forgotten her, and did not at once take in to what an important turn the affairs of some of us had come. She stepped out of the darkness, and put her hand on the door of the ambulance.

"I suppose you're the Paymaster?" Her voice was soft and easy, but had an ample volume. As Pidcock was replying with some dignity that she was correct, she caught sight of me. "Who is this man?" she interrupted him.

"My clerk," said Pidcock; and this is the promptest thing I can remember of the Major, always excepting his conduct when the firing began on the hill. "You're asking a good many questions, madam," he added.

"I want to know who I'm talking to," said she, quietly. "I think I've seen property of yours this evening."

"You had better get in, madam; better get in."

"This is the Paymaster's team from Fort Grant?" said Mrs. Sproud to the driver.

"Yes, yes, madam. Major Pidcock—I am Major Pidcock, Paymaster to the United States army in the Department of Colorado. I suppose I understand you."

"Seven canvas sacks," said Mrs. Sproud, standing in the road.

"Get in, madam. You can't tell who may be within hearing. You will find it to your advantage to keep nothing—"

Mrs. Sproud laughed luxuriously, and I began to discern why black curly might at times have been loath to face her.

151

"I merely meant, madam — I desired to make it clear that—a—"

"I think I know what you meant. But I have no call to fear the law. It will save you trouble to believe that before we go any further."

"Certainly, madam. Quite right." The man was sweating. What with court-martial and Mrs. Sproud, his withers were wrung. "You are entirely sure, of course, madam—"

"I am entirely sure I know what I am about. That seems to be more than some do that are interested in this gold—the folks, for instance, that have hid it in my hay-stack."

"Hay-stack! Then they're not gone to Mexico!"

"Mexico, sir? They live right here in this valley. Now I'll get in, and when I ask you, you will please to set me down." She seated herself opposite us and struck a match. "Now we know what we all look like," said she, holding the light up, massive and handsome. "This young man is the clerk, and we needn't mind him. I have done nothing to fear the law, but what I am doing now will make me a traveller again. I have no friends here. I was acquainted with a young man." She spoke in the serenest tone, but let fall the match more quickly than its burning made needful. "He was welcome in my home. He let them cook this up in my house and never told me. I live a good ways out on the road, and it was a safe place, but I didn't think why so many met him, and why they sat around my stable. Once in a while this week they've been joking about winning the soldiers' pay—they often win that—but I thought it was just cowboy games, till I heard horses coming quick at sundown this afternoon, and I hid. Will hunted

152

around and said—and said I was on the stage coming from Solomonsville, and so they had half an hour yet. He thought so. And, you see, nobody lives in the cabin but—but me." Mrs. Sproud paused a moment here, and I noticed her breathing. Then she resumed: "So I heard them talk some; and when they all left, pretty soon, I went to the hay-stack, and it was so. Then the stage came along and I rode to Thomas."

"You left the gold there !" groaned the wretched Major, and leaned out of the ambulance.

"I'm not caring to touch what's none of mine. Wait, sir, please; I get out here. Here are the names I'm sure of. Stop the driver, or I'll jump." She put a paper in the Major's hand. "It is Mrs. Sproud's hay-stack," she added.

"Will you—this will never—can I find you to-morrow ?" he said, helplessly, holding the paper out at her.

"I have told you all I know," said Mrs. Sproud, and was gone at once.

Major Pidcock leaned back for some moments as we drove. Then he began folding his paper with care. "I have not done with that person," said he, attempting to restore his crippled importance. "She will find that she must explain herself."

Our wheels whirled in the sand and we came quickly to Thomas, to a crowd of waiting officers and ladies; and each of us had an audience that night— the cook, I feel sure, while I myself was of an importance second only to the Major's. But he was at once closeted with the commanding officer, and I did not learn their counsels, hearing only at breakfast that the first step was taken. The detail sent out had

153

returned from the hay-stack, bringing gold indeed—
one-half sackful. The other six were gone, and so
was Mrs. Sproud. It was useless to surmise, as we.
however, did that whole forenoon, what any of this
might mean; but in the afternoon came a sign. A
citizen of the Gila Valley had been paying his many
debts at the saloon and through the neighborhood in
gold. In one well known for the past two years to
be without a penny it was the wrong moment to
choose for honest affluence, and this citizen was the
first arrest. This further instance of how secure the
robbers felt themselves to be outdid anything that
had happened yet, and I marvelled until following
events took from me the power of astonishment. The
men named on Mrs. Sproud's paper were fewer than
I think fired upon us in the attack, but every one of
them was here in the valley, going about his business.
Most were with the same herd of cattle that I had
seen driven by yellow and black curly near the sub-
agency, and they two were there. The solvent debtor,
I should say, was not arrested this morning. Plans
that I, of course, had no part in delayed matters, I
suppose for the sake of certainty. Black curly and
his friends were watched, and found to be spending
no gold yet; and since they did not show sign of
leaving the region, but continued with their cattle, I
imagine every effort was being made to light upon
their hidden treasure. But their time came, and soon
after it mine. Stirling, my friend, to whom I had
finally gone at Carlos, opened the wire door of his
quarters where I sat one morning, and with a heart-
less smile introduced me to a gentleman from Tucson.

"You'll have a chance to serve your country," said
Stirling.

I was subpœnaed!

"Certainly not!" I said, with indignation. "I'm going East. I don't live here. You have witnesses enough without me. We all saw the same thing."

"Witnesses never see the same thing," observed the man from Tucson. "It's the government that's after you. But you'll not have to wait. Our case is first on the list."

"You can take my deposition," I began; but what need to dwell upon this interview? "When I come to visit you again," I said to Stirling, "let me know." And that pink-faced, gray-haired captain still shouted heartlessly.

"You're an egotist," said he. "Think of the scrape poor old Pidcock has got himself into."

"The government needs all the witnesses it can get," said the man from Tucson. "Luke Jenks is smart in some ways."

"Luke Jenks?" I sat up in my canvas extension-chair.

"Territorial Delegate; firm of Parley and Jenks, Tucson. He's in it."

"By heavens!" I cried, in unmixed delight. "But I didn't see him when they were shooting at us."

The man from Tucson stared at me curiously. "He is counsel for the prisoners," he explained.

"The Delegate to Washington defends these thieves who robbed the United States?" I repeated.

"Says he'll get them off. He's going to stay home from Washington and put it through in shape."

It was here that my powers of astonishment went into their last decline, and I withheld my opinion upon the character of Mr. Jenks as a public man. I settled comfortably in my canvas chair.

155

"The prisoners are citizens of small means, I judge," said I. "What fee can they pay for such a service?"

"Ah!" said Stirling.

"That's about it, I guess," said the man from Tucson. "Luke is mighty smart in his law business. Well, gents, good-day to you. I must be getting after the rest of my witnesses."

"Have you seen Mrs. Sproud?" I asked him.

"She's quit the country. We can't trace her. Guess she was scared."

"But that gold!" I exclaimed, when Sterling and I were alone. "What in the world have they done with those six other bags?"

"Ah!" said he, as before. "Do you want to bet on that point? Dollars to doughnuts Uncle Sam never sees a cent of that money again. I'll stake my next quarter's pay—"

"Pooh!" said I. "That's poor odds against doughnuts if Pidcock has the paying of it." And I took my turn at laughing at the humorous Stirling.

"That Mrs. Sproud is a sensible woman to have gone," said he, reflectively. "They would know she had betrayed them, and she wouldn't be safe in the valley. Witnesses who know too much sometimes are found dead in this country—but you'll have government protection."

"Thank you kindly," said I. "That's what I had on the hill."

But Stirling took his turn at me again with freshened mirth.

Well, I think that we witnesses were worth government protection. At seasons of especial brightness and holiday, such as Christmas and Easter, the theatres of the variety order have a phrase which they

156

sometimes print in capitals upon their bills—Combination Extraordinary; and when you consider Major Pidcock and his pride, and the old plantation cook, and my reserved Eastern self, and our coal-black escort of the hill, more than a dozen, including Sergeant Brown and the private, both now happily recovered of their wounds, you can see what appearance we made descending together from the mean Southern Pacific train at Tucson, under the gaze of what I take to have been the town's whole population, numbering five thousand.

Stirling, who had come to see us through, began at his persiflage immediately, and congratulated me upon the house I should play to, speaking of box-office receipts and a benefit night. Tucson is more than half a Mexican town, and in its crowd upon the platform I saw the gaudy shawls, the ear-rings, the steeple straw hats, the old shrivelled cigarette-rolling apes, and the dark-eyed girls, and sifted with these the loungers of our own race, boots, overalls, pistols, hotel clerks, express agents, freight hands, waitresses, red-shirts, soldiers from Lowell Barracks, and officers, and in this mass and mess of color and dust and staring, Bishop Meakum, in his yellow duster, by the door of the Hotel San Xavier. But his stare was not, I think now, quite of the same idleness with the rest. He gave me a short nod, yet not unfriendly, as I passed by him to register my name. By the counter I found the wet-eyed Mowry standing.

"How's business on the other side of the track?" I said to him.

"Fair to middlin'. Get them mines ye was after at Globe?"

"You've forgotten I told you they're a property I

157

don't care for, Mr. Mowry. I suppose it's interest in this recent gold discovery that brings you to Tucson." He had no answer for me but a shrewd shirking glance that flattered my sense of acumen, and adding, pleasantly, "So many of your Arizona citizens have forsaken silver for gold just now," I wrote my name in the hotel book, while he looked to remind himself what it was.

"Why, you're not to stay here," said Stirling, coming up. "You're expected at the Barracks."

He presented me at once to a knot of officers, each of whom in turn made me known to some additional by-stander, until it seemed to me that I shook a new hand sixty times in this disordered minute by the hotel book, and out of the sixty caught one name, which was my own.

These many meetings could not be made perfect without help from the saloon - keeper, who ran his thriving trade conveniently at hand in the office of the San Xavier. Our group remained near him, and I silently resolved to sleep here at the hotel, away from the tempting confusion of army hospitality upon this eve of our trial. We were expected, however, to dine at the post, and that I was ready to do. Indeed, I could scarcely have got myself out of it without rudeness, for the ambulance was waiting us guests at the gate. We went to it along a latticed passage at the edge of a tropical garden, only a few square yards in all, but how pretty! and what an oasis of calm in the midst of this teeming desolation of unrest! It had upon one side the railway station, wooden, sordid, congesting with malodorous packed humanity; on the next the rails themselves and the platform, with steam and bells and baggage trucks rolling and bumping; the hotel stood on the third, a confusion of tongues and trampings; while a wide space of dust, knee-deep, and littered with manœuvring vehicles, hemmed in this silent garden on the fourth side. A slender slow little fountain dropped inaudibly among some palms, a giant cactus, and the broad-spread shade of trees I did not know. This was the whole garden, and a tame young antelope was its inhabitant. He lay in the unchanging shade, his large eyes fixed remotely upon the turmoil of this world, and a sleepy charm touched my senses as I looked at his domain. Instead of going to dinner, or going anywhere, I should have liked to recline indefinitely beneath those palms and trail my fingers in the cool fountain. Such enlightened languor, however, could by no happy chance be the lot of an important witness in a Western robbery trial, and I dined and wined with the jovial officers, at least talking no business.

With business I was sated. Pidcock and the attorney for the United States —I can remember neither his name nor the proper title of his office, for he was a nobody, and I had forgotten his features each new time that we met—had mapped out the trial to me, preparing and rehearsing me in my testimony until they had pestered me into a hatred of them both. And when word was brought me here, dining at Lowell Barracks, where I had imagined myself safe from justice, that this same attorney was waiting to see me, I rose and I played him a trick. Possibly I should not have done it but for the saloon-keeper in the afternoon and this sustained dining now; but I sent him word I should be with him directly—and I wandered into Tucson by myself!

159

Faithful to my last strong impression there, I went straight to the tiny hotel garden, and in that darkness lay down in a delicious and torpid triumph. The attorney was most likely waiting still. No one on earth knew where I was. Pidcock could not trace me now. I could see the stars through the palms and the strange trees, the fountain made a little sound, somewhere now and then I could hear the antelope, and, cloaked in this black serenity, I lay smiling. Once an engine passed heavily, leaving the station utterly quiet again, and the next I knew it was the antelope's rough tongue that waked me, and I found him nibbling and licking my hand. People were sitting in the latticed passage, and from the light in the office came Mr. Mowry, untying a canvas sack that he held. At this sight my truancy to discretion was over, and no head could be more wakeful or clear than mine instantly became.

"How much d'yer want this time, Mr. Jenks?" inquired Mowry.

I could not hear the statesman's reply, but thought, while the sound of clinking came to me, how a common cause will often serve to reconcile the most bitter opponents. I did not dare go nearer to catch all their talk, and I debated a little upon my security even as it was, until my own name suddenly reached me.

"Him?" said Mowry; "that there tailor-made boy? They've got him sleepin' at the Barracks."

"Nobody but our crowd's boarding here," said some one.

"They think we're laying for their witnesses," said the voice of Jenks. And among the various mingled laughs rose distinct a big one that I knew.

"Oh, ho, ho! Well, yes. Tell you about witnesses.

160

Here's all there is to them: spot cash to their figure, and kissing the Book. You've done no work but what I told you?" he added, sharply.

"We haven't needed to worry about witnesses in any shape, Bishop."

"That's good. That's economy. That little Eastern toorist is harmless."

"Leave him talk, Bishop. Leave 'em all tell their story."

"It's going to cost the whole stake, though," said Jenks.

"Deserted Jericho!" remarked old Meakum.

"I don't try cases for nothing, Bishop. The deal's covered. My clients have publicly made over to me their horses and saddles."

"Oh, ho, ho!" went the Bishop. But this last word about the horses was the only part of the talk I could not put a plain meaning upon.

Mr. Mowry I now saw re-enter the lighted door of the office, with his canvas sack in his hand. "This 'll be right here in the safe," said he.

"All right," answered Jenks. "I'll not be likely to call on you any more for a day or so."

"Hello!" said the office clerk, appearing in his shirt-sleeves. "You fellows have made me forget the antelope." He took down a lantern, and I rose to my feet.

"Give us a drink before you feed him," said Jenks. Then I saw the whole of them crowd into the door for their nightcap, and that was all I waited for.

I climbed the garden fence. My thoughts led me at random through quantities of soft dust, and over the rails, I think, several times, until I stood between empty and silent freight trains, and there sat down.

161

Harmless! It seemed to me they would rate me differently in the morning. So for a while my mind was adrift in the turbulent cross-currents of my discovery; but it was with a smooth, innocent surface that I entered the hotel office and enjoyed the look of the clerk when he roused and heard me, who, according to their calculations, should have been in slumber at the Barracks, asking to be shown my room here. I was tempted to inquire if he had fed the antelope— such was the pride of my elation—and I think he must have been running over questions to put me; but the two of us marched up the stairs with a lamp and a key, speaking amiably of the weather for this time of year, and he unlocked my door with a politeness and hoped I would sleep well with a consideration that I have rarely met in the hotel clerk. I did not sleep well. Yet it seemed not to matter. By eight I had breakfast, and found the attorney—Rocklin I shall name him, and that will have to answer—and told him how we had become masters of the situation.

He made me repeat it all over, jotting memoranda this second time; and when my story was done, he sat frowning at his notes, with a cigar between his teeth.

"This ain't much," he said. "Luckily I don't need anything more. I've got a dead open-and-shut case without it."

"Why don't you make it deader, then?" said I. "Don't you see what it all means?"

"Well, what does it all mean?"

Either the man was still nettled at my treatment of him last evening, or had no liking for amateur opinions and help; otherwise I see no reason for the disparagement with which he regarded me while I interpreted what I had overheard, piece by piece, except the horse and saddle remark.

"Since that don't seem clear, I'll explain it to you," he said, "and then you'll know it all. Except their horses and saddles, the accused haven't a red cent to their names—not an honest one, that is. So it looks well for them to be spending all they've apparently got in the world to pay counsel fees. Now I have this case worked up," he pursued, complacently, "so that any such ambiguous stuff as yours is no good to me at all—would be harmful, in fact. It's not good policy, my friend, to assail the character of opposing counsel. And Bishop Meakum! Are you aware of his power and standing in this section? Do you think you're going to ring him in?"

"Great goodness!" I cried. "Let me testify, and then let the safe be opened."

Rocklin looked at me a moment, the cigar wagging between his teeth, and then he lightly tossed his notes in the waste-paper basket.

"Open your safe," said he, "and what then? Up steps old Mowry and says, 'I'll thank you to let my property alone.' Where's your proof? What word did any of them drop that won't bear other constructions? Mowry's well known to have money, and he has a right to give it to Jenks."

"If the gold could be identified?" I suggested.

"That's been all attended to," he answered, with increasing complacence. "I'm obliged to you for your information, and in a less sure case I might risk using it, but—why, see here; we've got 'em hands down!" And he clapped me on the knee. "If I had met you last evening I was going to tell you our campaign. Pidcock 'll come first, of course, and his testimony 'll

163

cover pretty much the whole ground. Then, you see, the rest of you I'll use mainly in support. Sergeant Brown—he's very strong, and the black woman, and you—I'll probably call you third or fourth. So you'll be on hand sure now?"

Certainly I had no thought of being anywhere else. The imminence of our trial was now heralded by the cook's coming to Rocklin's office punctual to his direction, and after her Pidcock almost immediately. It was not many minutes before the more important ones of us had gathered, and we proceeded to court, once again a Combination Extraordinary—a spectacle for Tucson. So much stir and prosperity had not blossomed in the town for many years, its chief source of life being the money that Lowell Barracks brought to it. But now its lodgings were crowded and its saloons and Mexican dens of entertainment waked to activity. From a dozing sunburnt village of adobe walls and almond‑trees it was become something like those places built in a single Western day of riot extravagance, where corner lots are clamored for and men pay a dollar to be shaved.

Jenks was before us in the room with his clients. He was practising what I always think of as his celluloid smile, whispering, and all-hail with everybody. One of the prisoners had just such another mustache as his own, too large for his face; and this had led me since to notice a type of too large mustaches through our country in all ranks, but of similar men, who generally have either stolen something or lacked the opportunity. Catching sight of me, Jenks came at once, friendly as you please, shaking my passive hand, and laughing that we should meet again under such circumstances.

164

"When we're through this nuisance," said he, "you must take dinner with me. Just now, you understand, it wouldn't look well to see me hobnobbing with a government witness. See you again!" And he was off to some one else.

I am confident this man could not see himself as others—some others, at least—saw him. To him his whole performance was natural and professional, and my view that he was more infamous by far than the thieves would have sincerely amazed him. Indeed, for one prisoner I felt very sorry. Young black curly was sitting there, and, in contrast to Mr. Adams, down whose beard the tobacco forever ran, he seemed downcast and unhardened, I thought. He was getting his deserts through base means. It was not for the sake of justice but from private revenge that Mrs. Sproud had moved; and, after all, had the boy injured her so much as this? Yet how could I help him? They were his deserts. My mood was abruptly changed to diversion when I saw among our jury specimens of both types of Meakum, and prominent among the spectator throng their sire, that canny polygamist, surveying the case with the same forceful attention I had noticed first in the House of Representatives, and ever since that day. But I had a true shock of surprise now. Mrs. Sproud was in court. There could be no mistake. No one seemed to notice her, and I wondered if many in the town knew her face, and with what intent she had returned to this dangerous neighborhood. I was so taken up with watching her and her furtive appearance in the almost concealed position she had chosen that I paid little heed to the government's opening of its case. She had her eyes upon black curly, but he could not

165

see her. Pidcock was in the midst of his pompous recital when the court took its noon intermission. Then I was drawn to seek out black curly as he was conducted to his dinner.

"Good-day," said he, as I came beside him.

"I wish I didn't have to go on oath about this," I said.

"Oath away," he answered, doggedly. "What's that got to do with me?"

"Oh, come!" I exclaimed.

"Come where?" He looked at me defiantly.

"When people don't wish to be trailed," I went on, "do I understand they sometimes spread a blanket and lead their horses on it and take off their shoes? I'm merely asking out of a traveller's curiosity."

"I guess you'll have to ask them that's up on such tricks," he answered, grinning.

I met him in the eyes, and a strong liking for him came over me. "I probably owe you my life," I said, huskily. "I know I do. And I hate—you must consider me a poor sort of bird."

"Blamed if I know what you're drivin' at," said black curly. But he wrinkled his forehead in the pleasant way I remembered. "Yer whiskey was good all right," he added, and gave me his hand.

"Look here," said I. "She's come back."

This took the boy unguarded, and he swore with surprise. Then his face grew sombre. "Let her," he remarked; and that was all we said.

At the afternoon sitting I began to notice how popular sympathy was not only quite against the United States, but a sentiment amounting to hatred was shown against all soldiers. The voice of respectability seemed entirely silent; decent citizens were

166

there, but not enough of them. The mildest opinion was that Uncle Sam could afford to lose money better than poor people, and the strongest was that it was a pity the soldiers had not been killed. This seemed inappropriate in a Territory desiring admission to our Union. I supposed it something local then, but have since observed it to be a prevailing Western antipathy. The unthinking sons of the sage-brush ill tolerate a thing which stands for discipline, good order, and obedience, and the man who lets another command him they despise. I can think of no threat more evil for our democracy, for it is a fine thing diseased and perverted—namely, independence gone drunk.

Pidcock's examination went forward, and the half-sack of gold from the hay-stack brought a great silence in court. The Major's identification of the gold was conducted by Rocklin with stage effect, for it was an undoubted climax; but I caught a most singular smile on the face of Bishop Meakum, and there sat Mrs. Sproud, still solitary and engulfed in the throng, her face flushed and her eyes blazing. And here ended the first day.

In the morning came the Major's cross-examination, with the room more crowded than before, but I could not find Mrs. Sproud. Rocklin did not believe I had seen her, and I feared something had happened to her. The Bishop had walked to the court with Jenks, talking and laughing upon general subjects, so far as I could hear. The counsel for the prisoners passed lightly over the first part of the evidence, only causing an occasional laugh on the score of the Major's military prowess, until he came to the gold.

"You said this sack was one of yours, Major?" he now inquired.

"It is mine, sir."

A large bundle of sacks was brought. "And how about these? Here are ten, fifteen—about forty. I'll get some more if you say so. Are they all yours?"

"Your question strikes me as idle, sir." The court rapped, and Jenks smiled. "They resemble mine," said Pidcock. "But they are not used."

"No; not used." Jenks held up the original, shaking the gold. "Now I'm going to empty your sack for a moment."

"I object," said Rocklin, springing up.

"Oh, it's all counted," laughed Jenks; and the objection was not sustained. Then Jenks poured the gold into a new sack and shook that aloft. "It makes them look confusingly similar, Major. I'll just put my card in your sack."

"I object," said Rocklin, with anger, but with futility. Jenks now poured the gold back into the first, then into a third, and thus into several, tossing them each time on the table, and the clinking pieces sounded clear in the room. Bishop Meakum was watching the operation like a wolf. "Now, Major," said Jenks, "is your gold in the original sack, or which sack is my card in?"

This was the first time that the room broke out loudly; and Pidcock, when the people were rapped to order, said, "The sack's not the thing."

"Of course not. The gold is our point. And of course you had a private mark on it. Tell the jury, please, what the private mark was."

He had none. He spoke about dates, and new coins, he backed and filled, swelled importantly, and ended like a pricked bladder by recanting his identification.

"That is all I have to say for the present," said Jenks.

"Don't complicate the issue by attempting to prove too much, Mr. Rocklin," said the judge.

Rocklin flushed, and called the next witness, whispering sulkily to me, "What can you expect if the court starts out against you?" But the court was by no means against him. The judge was merely disgusted over Rocklin's cardinal folly of identifying coin under such loose conditions.

And now came the testimony of Sergeant Brown. He told so clear a story as to chill the enthusiasm of the room. He pointed to the man with the mustache, black curly, and yellow. "I saw them shooting from the right of the road," he said. Jenks tried but little to shake him, and left him unshaken. He was followed by the other wounded soldier, whose story was nearly the same, except that he identified different prisoners.

"Who did you say shot you?" inquired Jenks. "Which of these two?"

"I didn't say. I don't know."

"Don't know a man when he shoots you in broad daylight?"

"Plenty was shooting at me," said the soldier. And his testimony also remained unshaken.

Then came my own examination, and Jenks did not trouble me at all, but, when I had likewise identified the men I knew, simply bowed smilingly, and had no questions to ask his friend from the East.

Our third morning began with the negress, who said she was married, told a scattered tale, and soon stated that she was single, explaining later that she had two husbands, and one was dead, while the other had dis-

169

appeared from her ten years ago. Gradually her alarm subsided and she achieved coherence.

"What did this gentleman do at the occurrence?" inquired Jenks, indicating me.

"Dat gemman? He jes flew, sir, an' I don' blame him fo' bein' no wusser skeer'd dan de hole party. Yesser, we all flew scusin' dey two pore chillun; an' we stayed till de 'currence was ceased."

"But the gentleman says he sat on a stone, and saw those men firing."

"Land! I seed him goin' like he was gwineter Fo't Grant. He run up de hill, an' de Gennul he run down like de day of judgment."

"The General ran?"

"Lawd grashus, honey, yo' could have played checkers on dey coat tails of his."

The court rapped gently.

"But the gold must have been heavy to carry away to the horses. Did not the General exert his influence to rally his men?"

"No, sah. De Gennul went down de hill, an' he took his inflooence with him."

"I have no further questions," said Jenks. "When we come to our alibis, gentlemen, I expect to satisfy you that this lady saw more correctly, and when she is unable to recognize my clients it is for a good reason."

"We've not got quite so far yet," Rocklin observed. "We've reached the hay-stack at present."

"Aren't you going to make her describe her own confusion more?" I began, but stopped, for I saw that the next witness was at hand, and that it was Mrs. Sproud.

"How's this?" I whispered to Rocklin. "How did you get her?"

170

"She volunteered this morning, just before trial. We're in big luck."

The woman was simply dressed in something dark. Her handsome face was pale, but she held a steady eye upon the jury, speaking clearly and with deliberation. Old Meakum, always in court and watchful, was plainly unprepared for this, and among the prisoners, too, I could discern uneasiness. Whether or no any threat or constraint had kept her invisible during these days, her coming now was a thing for which none of us were ready.

"What do I know?" she repeated after the counsel. "I suppose you have been told what I said I knew."

"We'd like to hear it directly from you, Mrs. Sproud," Rocklin explained.

"Where shall I start?"

"Well, there was a young man who boarded with you, was there not?"

"I object to the witness being led," said Jenks. And Bishop Meakum moved up beside the prisoners' counsel and began talking with him earnestly.

"Nobody is leading me," said Mrs. Sproud, imperiously, and raising her voice a little. She looked about her. "There was a young man who boarded with me. Of course that is so."

Meakum broke off in his confidences with Jenks, and looked sharply at her.

"Do you see your boarder anywhere here?" inquired Rocklin; and from his tone I perceived that he was puzzled by the manner of his witness.

She turned slowly, and slowly scrutinized the prisoners one by one. The head of black curly was bent down, and I saw her eyes rest upon it while she stood

171

in silence. It was as if he felt the summons of her glance, for he raised his head. His face was scarlet, but her paleness did not change.

"He is the one sitting at the end," she said, looking back at the jury. She then told some useless particulars, and brought her narrative to the afternoon when she had heard the galloping. "Then I hid. I hid because this is a rough country."

"When did you recognize that young man's voice?"

"I did not recognize it."

Black curly's feet scraped as he shifted his position.

"Collect yourself, Mrs. Sproud. We'll give you all the time you want. We know ladies are not used to talking in court. Did you not hear this young man talking to his friends?"

"I heard talking," replied the witness, quite collected. "But I could not make out who they were. If I could have been sure it was him and friends, I wouldn't have stayed hid. I'd have had no call to be scared."

Rocklin was dazed, and his next question came in a voice still more changed and irritable.

"Did you see any one?"

"No one."

"What did you hear them say?"

"They were all talking at once. I couldn't be sure."

"Why did you go to the hay-stack?"

"Because they said something about my hay-stack, and I wanted to find out, if I could."

"Did you not write their names on a paper and give it to this gentleman? Remember you are on oath, Mrs. Sproud."

By this time a smile was playing on the features of

172

Jenks, and he and Bishop Meakum talked no longer together, but sat back to watch the woman's extraordinary attempt to undo her work. It was shrewd, very shrewd, in her to volunteer as our witness instead of as theirs. She was ready for the paper question, evidently.

"I wrote—" she began, but Rocklin interrupted.

"On oath, remember!" he repeated, finding himself cross-examining his own witness. "The names you wrote are the names of these prisoners here before the court. They were traced as the direct result of your information. They have been identified by three or four persons. Do you mean to say you did not know who they were?"

"I did not know," said Mrs. Sproud, firmly. "As for the paper, I acted hasty. I was a woman, alone, and none to consult or advise me. I thought I would get in trouble if I did not tell about such goings on, and I just wrote the names of Will—of the boys that came round there all the time, thinking it was most likely them. I didn't see him, and I didn't make out surely it was his voice. I wasn't sure enough to come out and ask what they were up to. I didn't stop to think of the harm I was doing on guesswork."

For the first time the note of remorse conquered in her voice. I saw how desperation at what she had done when she thought her love was cured was now bracing the woman to this audacity.

"Remember," said Rocklin, "the gold was also found as the direct result of your information. It was you who told Major Pidcock in the ambulance about the seven sacks."

"I never said anything about seven sacks."

This falsehood was a master-stroke, for only half a sack had been found. She had not written this down. There was only the word of Pidcock and me to vouch for it, while against us stood her denial, and the actual quantity of gold.

"I have no further questions," said Rocklin.

"But I have," said Jenks. And then he made the most of Mrs. Sproud, although many in the room were laughing, and she herself, I think, felt she had done little but sacrifice her own character without repairing the injury she had done black curly. Jenks made her repeat that she was frightened; not calm enough to be sure of voices, especially many speaking together; that she had seen no one throughout. He even attempted to show that the talk about the hay-stack might have been purely about hay, and that the half-sack of gold might have been put there at another time—might belong to some honest man this very moment.

"Did you ever know the young man who boarded with you to do a dishonorable thing?" inquired Jenks. "Did you not have the highest opinion of him?"

She had not expected a question like this. It nearly broke the woman down. She put her hand to her breast, and seemed afraid to trust her voice. "I have the highest opinion of him," she said, word painfully following word. "He—he used to know that."

"I have finished," said Jenks.

"Can I go?" asked the witness, and the attorneys bowed. She stood one hesitating moment in the witness-stand, and she looked at the jury and the court; then, as if almost in dread, she let her eyes travel to black curly. But his eyes were sullenly averted. Then Mrs. Sproud slowly made her way

174

through the room, with one of the saddest faces I have ever seen, and the door closed behind her.

We finished our case with all the prisoners identified, and some of them doubly. The defence was scarcely more than a sham. The flimsy alibis were destroyed even by the incompetent, unready Rocklin, and when the charge came blackness fell upon the citizens of Tucson. The judge's cold statements struck them as partisan, and they murmured and looked darkly at him. But the jury, with its Meakums, wore no expression at all during any of his remarks. Their eyes were upon him, but entirely fish-like. He dismissed the cumbersome futilities one by one. "Now three witnesses have between them recognized all the prisoners but one," he continued. "That one, a reputed pauper, paid several hundred dollars of debts in gold the morning after the robbery. The money is said to be the proceeds of a cattle sale. No cattle have ever been known to belong to this man, and the purchaser had never been known to have any income until this trial began. The prisoner's name was on Mrs. Sproud's paper. The statement of one witness that he sat on a stone and saw three other of the prisoners firing has been contradicted by a woman who described herself as having run away at once; it is supported by two men who are admitted by all to have remained, and in consequence been shot. Their statements have been assailed by no one. Their testimony stands on the record unimpeached. They have identified five prisoners. If you believe them—and remember that not a word they said has been questioned—" here the judge emphasized more and more clearly. He concluded with the various alternatives of fact according

175

to which the jury must find its several possible verdicts. When he had finished, the room sat sullen and still, and the twelve went out. I am told that they remained ten minutes away. It seemed one to me.

When they had resumed their seats I noticed the same fishlike oracular eye in most of them unchanged. "Not guilty," said the foreman.

"What!" shouted the judge, startled out of all judicial propriety. "None of 'em?"

"Not guilty," monotonously repeated the foreman.

We were silent amid the din of triumph now raised by Tucson. In the laughter, the hand-shaking, the shouting, and the jubilant pistol-shots that some particularly free spirit fired in the old Cathedral Square, we went to our dinner; and not even Stirling could joke. "There's a certain natural justice done here in spite of them," he said. "They are not one cent richer for all their looted twenty-eight thousand. They come out free, but penniless."

"How about Jenks and that jury?" said I. And Stirling shrugged his shoulders.

But we had yet some crowning impudence to learn. Later, in the street, the officers and I met the prisoners, their witnesses, and their counsel emerging from a photographer's studio. The Territorial Delegate had been taken in a group with his acquitted thieves. The Bishop had declined to be in this souvenir.

"That's a picture I want," said I. "Only I'll be sorry to see your face there," I added to black curly.

"Indeed!" put in Jenks.

"Yes," said I. "You and he do not belong in the same class. By-the-way, Mr. Jenks, I suppose you'll return their horses and saddles now?"

176

Too many were listening for him to lose his temper, and he did a sharp thing. He took this public opportunity for breaking some news to his clients. " I had hoped to," he said ; "that is, as many as were not needed to defray necessary costs. But it's been an expensive suit, and I've found myself obliged to sell them all. It's little enough to pay for clearing your character, boys."

They saw through his perfidy to them, and that he had them checkmated. Any protest from them would be a confession of their theft. Yet it seemed an unsafe piece of villany in Jenks.

" They look disappointed," I remarked. " I shall value the picture very highly."

" If that's Eastern sarcasm," said Jenks, "it's beyond me."

" No, Mr. Jenks," I answered. " In your presence sarcasm drops dead. I think you'll prosper in politics."

But there I was wrong. There is some natural justice in these events, though I wish there were more. The jury, it is true, soon seemed oddly prosperous as Stirling wrote me afterwards. They painted their houses ; two of them, who had generally walked before, now had wagons ; and in so many of their gardens and small ranches did the plants and fruits increase that, as Stirling put it, they had evidently sowed their dollars. But upon Jenks Territorial displeasure did descend. He had stayed away too much from Washington. A pamphlet appeared with the title, " What Luke Jenks Has Done for Arizona." Inside were twenty blank pages, and he failed of re-election.

Furthermore, the government retaliated upon this district by abandoning Camp Thomas and Lowell

Barracks, those important sources of revenue for the neighborhood. The brief boom did not help Tucson very long, and left it poorer than ever.

At the station I saw Mrs. Sproud and black curly, neither speaking to the other. It was plain that he had utterly done with her, and that she was too proud even to look at him. She went West, and he as far east as Willcox. Neither one have I ever seen again.

But I have the photograph, and I sometimes wonder what has happened to black curly. Arizona is still a Territory; and when I think of the Gila Valley and of the Boy Orator, I recall Bishop Meakum's remark about our statesmen at Washington: "You can divide them birds in two lots—those who know better, and those who don't. D'you follow me?"

Padre Ignazio

AT Santa Ysabel del Mar the season was at
one of its moments when the air hangs
quiet over land and sea. The old breezes
had gone; the new ones were not yet risen.
The flowers in the mission garden opened wide,
for no wind came by day or night to shake the
loose petals from their stems. Along the bask-
ing, silent, many-colored shore gathered and
lingered the crisp odors of the mountains.
The dust floated golden and motionless long
after the rider was behind the hill, and the
Pacific lay like a floor of sapphire, on which to
walk beyond the setting sun into the East.
One white sail shone there. Instead of an
hour, it had been from dawn till afternoon in
sight between the short headlands; and the
padre had hoped that it might be his ship.
But it had slowly passed. Now from an arch
in his garden cloisters he was watching the
last of it. Presently it was gone, and the great
ocean lay empty. The padre put his glasses in

his lap. For a short while he read in his breviary, but soon forgot it again. He looked at the flowers and sunny ridges, then at the huge blue triangle of sea which the opening of the hills let into sight. "Paradise," he murmured, "need not hold more beauty and peace. But I think I would exchange all my remaining years of this for one sight again of Paris or Seville. May God forgive me such a thought!"

Across the unstirred fragrance of oleanders the bell for vespers began to ring. Its tones passed over the padre as he watched the sea in his garden. They reached his parishioners in their adobe dwellings near by. The gentle circles of sound floated outward upon the smooth immense silence—over the vines and pear-trees ; down the avenues of the olives ; into the planted fields, whence women and children began to return ; then out of the lap of the valley along the yellow uplands, where the men that rode among the cattle paused, looking down like birds at the map of their home. Then the sound widened, faint, unbroken, until it met Temptation riding towards the padre from the south, and cheered the steps of Temptation's jaded horse.

"For a day, one single day of Paris !" repeated the padre, gazing through his cloisters at the empty sea.

182

Once in the year the mother-world remembered him. Once in the year a barkentine came sailing with news and tokens from Spain. It was in 1685 that a galleon had begun such voyages up to the lower country from Acapulco, where she loaded the cargo that had come across Tehuantepec on mules from Vera Cruz. By 1768 she had added the new mission of San Diego to her ports. In the year that we, a thin strip of colonists away over on the Atlantic edge of the continent, declared ourselves an independent nation, that Spanish ship, in the name of Saint Francis, was unloading the centuries of her own civilization at the Golden Gate. Then, slowly, as mission after mission was planted along the soft coast wilderness, she made new stops—at Santa Barbara, for instance ; and by Point San Luis for San Luis Obispo, that lay inland a little way up the gorge where it opened among the hills. Thus the world reached these places by water ; while on land, through the mountains, a road came to lead to them, and also to many more that were too distant behind the hills for ships to serve—a long, lonely, rough road, punctuated with church towers and gardens. For the fathers gradually so stationed their settlements that the traveller might each morning ride out from one mission and by evening of a day's fair journey ride into the next. A long, rough road; and in its way pretty to think of now.

So there, by-and-by, was our continent, with the locomotive whistling from Savannah to Boston along its eastern edge, and on the other the scattered chimes of Spain ringing among the unpeopled mountains. Thus grew the two sorts of civilization—not equally. We know what has happened since. To-day the locomotive is whistling also from the Golden Gate to San Diego; but the old mission road goes through the mountains still, and on it the steps of vanished Spain are marked with roses, and white cloisters, and the crucifix.

But this was 1855. Only the barkentine brought the world that he loved to the padre. As for the new world which was making a rude noise to the northward, he trusted that it might keep away from Santa Ysabel, and he waited for the vessel that was overdue with its package containing his single worldly indulgence.

As the little, ancient bronze bell continued its swinging in the tower, its plaintive call reached something in the padre's memory. Without knowing, he began to sing. He took up the slow strain not quite correctly, and dropped it, and took it up again, always in cadence with the bell:

184

At length he heard himself, and glancing at the belfry, smiled a little. "It is a pretty tune," he said, "and it always made me sorry for poor Fra Diavolo. Auber himself confessed to me that he had made it sad and put the hermitage bell to go with it because he too was grieved at having to kill his villain, and wanted him to die, if possible, in a religious frame of mind. And Auber touched glasses with me and said—how well I remember it!— 'Is it the good Lord, or is it merely the devil, that makes me always have a weakness for rascals?' I told him it was the devil. I was not a priest then. I could not be so sure with my answer now." And then Padre Ignazio repeated Auber's remark in French: "'Est-ce le bon Dieu, ou est-ce bien le diable, qui me fait toujours aimer les coquins?' I don't know! I don't know! I wonder if Auber has composed anything lately? I wonder who is singing Zerlina now?"

He cast a farewell look at the ocean, and took his steps between the monastic herbs and the oleanders to the sacristy. "At least," he said, "if we cannot carry with us into exile the friends and the places that we have loved, music will go where we go, even to such an end of the world as this. Felipe!" he called to his organist. "Can they sing the music I taught them for the Dixit Dominus to-night?"

"Yes, father, surely."

"Then we will have that. And, Felipe—" The padre crossed the chancel to the small shabby organ. "Rise, my child, and listen. Here is something you can learn. Why, see now if you cannot learn it with a single hearing."

The swarthy boy of sixteen stood watching his master's fingers, delicate and white, as they played. So of his own accord he had begun to watch them when a child of six; and the padre had taken the wild, half-scared, spellbound creature and made a musician of him.

"There, Felipe!" he said now. "Can you do it? Slower, and more softly, *muchacho*. It is about the death of a man, and it should go with our bell."

The boy listened. "Then the father has played it a tone too low," said he; "for our bell rings the note of *sol*, or something very near it, as the father must surely know." He placed the melody in the right key—an easy thing for him; but the padre was delighted.

"Ah, my Felipe," he exclaimed, "what could you and I not do if we had a better organ! Only a little better! See! above this row of keys would be a second row, and many more stops. Then we would make such music as has never been heard in California yet. But my people are so poor and so few! And some day I shall have passed from them, and it will be too late."

"Perhaps," ventured Felipe, "the Americanos—"

"They care nothing for us, Felipe. They are not of our religion — or of any religion, from what I can hear. Don't forget my Dixit Dominus." And the padre retired once more to the sacristy, while the horse that carried Tempation came over the hill.

The hour of service drew near; and as he waited, the padre once again stepped out for a look at the ocean; but the blue triangle of water lay like a picture in its frame of land, empty as the sky. "I think, from the color, though," said he, "that a little more wind must have begun out there."

The bell rang a last short summons to prayer. Along the road from the south a young rider, leading one pack-animal, ambled into the mission and dismounted. Church was not so much in his thoughts as food and, in due time after that, a bed; but the doors stood open, and as everybody was going into them, more variety was to be gained by joining this company than by waiting outside alone until they should return from their devotions. So he seated himself at the back, and after a brief, jaunty glance at the sunburnt, shaggy congregation, made himself as comfortable as might be. He had not seen a face worth keeping his eyes open for. The simple choir and simple fold gathered for even-song, and paid him no attention on their part — a rough American bound for the mines was no longer anything but an object of aversion to them.

The padre, of course, had been instantly aware of the stranger's presence. For this is the sixth sense with vicars of every creed and heresy; and if the parish is lonely and the worshippers few and seldom varying, a newcomer will gleam out like a new book to be read. And a trained priest learns to read shrewdly the faces of those who assemble to worship under his guidance. But American vagrants, with no thoughts save of gold-digging, and an overweening illiterate jargon for their speech, had long ceased to interest this priest, even in his starvation for company and talk from the outside world; and therefore after the intoning, he sat with his homesick thoughts unchanged, to draw both pain and enjoyment from the music that he had set to the Dixit Dominus. He listened to the tender chorus that opens " William Tell "; and as the Latin psalm proceeded, pictures of the past rose between him and the altar. One after another came these strains which he had taken from the operas famous in their day, until at length the padre was murmuring to some music seldom long out of his heart—not the Latin verse which the choir sang, but the original French words:

> Ah, voilà mon envie,
>   Voilà mon seul désir:
> Rendez moi ma patrie,
>   Ou laissez moi mourir.

Which may be rendered:

> One only wish I know,
>   One word is all my cry:
> Give back my native land to me,
>   Give back, or let me die.

Then it happened that he saw the stranger in the back of the church again, and forgot his Dixit Dominus straightway. The face of the young man was no longer hidden by the slouching position he had at first taken. "I only noticed his clothes before," thought the padre. Restlessness was plain upon the handsome brow, and in the mouth there was violence; but Padre Ignazio liked the eyes. "He is not saying any prayers," he surmised, presently. "I doubt if he has said any for a long while. And he knows my music. He is of educated people. He cannot be American. And now—yes, he has taken—I think it must be a flower, from his pocket. I shall have him to dine with me." And vespers ended with rosy clouds of eagerness drifting across the padre's brain.

But the stranger made his own beginning. As the priest came from the church, the rebellious young figure was waiting. "Your organist tells me," he said, impetuously, "that it is you who—"

"May I ask with whom I have the great pleasure of speaking?" said the padre, putting formality to the front and his pleasure out of sight.

The stranger reddened, and became aware of the padre's features, moulded by refinement and the world. "I beg your lenience," said he, with a graceful and confident utterance, as of equal to equal. "My name is Gaston

Villeré, and it was time I should be reminded of my manners."

The padre's hand waved a polite negative.

"Indeed yes, padre. But your music has astonished me to pieces. If you carried such associations as— Ah! the days and the nights!" he broke off. "To come down a California mountain," he resumed, "and find Paris at the bottom! 'The Huguenots,' Rossini, Hérold— I was waiting for 'Il Trovatore.'"

"Is that something new?" said the padre, eagerly.

The young man gave an exclamation. "The whole world is ringing with it," he said.

"But Santa Ysabel del Mar is a long way from the whole world," said Padre Ignazio.

"Indeed it would not appear to be so," returned young Gaston. "I think the Comédie Française must be round the corner."

A thrill went through the priest at the theatre's name. "And have you been long in America?" he asked.

"Why, always—except two years of foreign travel after college."

"An American!" said the surprised padre, with perhaps a flavor of disappointment in his voice. "But no Americans who have yet come this way have been—have been"—he veiled the too blunt expression of his thought—"have been familiar with 'The Huguenots,'" he finished, making a slight bow.

Villeré took his under-meaning. "I come from New Orleans," he returned. "And in New Orleans there live many of us who can recognize a—who can recognize good music wherever we meet it." And he made a slight bow in his turn.

The padre laughed outright with pleasure, and laid his hand upon the young man's arm. "You have no intention of going away tomorrow, I trust?" said he.

"With your leave," answered Gaston, "I will have such an intention no longer."

It was with the air and gait of mutual understanding that the two now walked on together towards the padre's door. The guest was twenty-five, the host sixty.

"And have you been in America long?" inquired Gaston.

"Twenty years."

"And at Santa Ysabel how long?"

"Twenty years."

"I should have thought," said Gaston, looking lightly at the empty mountains, "that now and again you might have wished to travel."

"Were I your age," murmured Padre Ignazio, "it might be so."

The evening had now ripened to the long

after-glow of sunset. The sea was the purple of grapes, and wine-colored hues flowed among the high shoulders of the mountains.

"I have seen a sight like this," said Gaston, "between Granada and Malaga."

"So you know Spain!" said the padre.

Often he had thought of this resemblance, but never heard it told to him before. The courtly proprietor of San Fernando, and the other patriarchal rancheros with whom he occasionally exchanged visits across the wilderness, knew hospitality and inherited gentle manners, sending to Europe for silks and laces to give their daughters; but their eyes had not looked upon Granada, and their ears had never listened to "William Tell."

"It is quite singular," pursued Gaston, "how one nook in the world will suddenly remind you of another nook that may be thousands of miles away. One morning, behind the Quai Voltaire, an old yellow house with rusty balconies made me almost homesick for New Orleans."

"The Quai Voltaire!" said the padre.

"I heard Rachel in 'Valeria' that night," the young man went on. "Did you know that she could sing too? She sang several verses by an astonishing little Jew musician that has come up over there."

The padre gazed down at his blithe guest. "To see somebody, somebody, once again," he said, "is very pleasant to a hermit."

"It cannot be more pleasant than arriving at an oasis," returned Gaston.

They had delayed on the threshold to look at the beauty of the evening, and now the priest watched his parishioners come and go. "How can one make companions—" he began; then, checking himself, he said: "Their souls are as sacred and immortal as mine, and God helps me to help them. But in this world it is not immortal souls that we choose for companions; it is kindred tastes, intelligences, and—and so I and my books are growing old together, you see," he added, more lightly. "You will find my volumes as behind the times as myself."

He had fallen into talk more intimate than he wished; and while the guest was uttering something polite about the nobility of missionary work, he placed him in an easy-chair and sought *aguardiente* for his immediate refreshment. Since the year's beginning there had been no guest for him to bring into his rooms, or to sit beside him in the high seats at table, set apart for the *gente fina*.

Such another library was not then in California; and though Gaston Villeré, in leaving Harvard College, had shut Horace and Sophocles forever at the earliest instant possible under academic requirements, he knew the Greek and Latin names that he now saw as well as he knew those of Shakespeare, Dante, Molière, and Cervantes. These were here also; nor could it be precisely said of them, either, that they made a part of the young man's daily reading. As he surveyed the padre's august shelves, it was with a touch of the florid Southern gravity which his Northern education had not wholly schooled out of him that he said:

"I fear that I am no scholar, sir. But I know what writers every gentleman ought to respect."

The subtle padre bowed gravely to this compliment.

It was when his eyes caught sight of the music that the young man felt again at ease, and his vivacity returned to him. Leaving his chair, he began enthusiastically to examine the tall piles that filled one side of the room. The volumes lay richly everywhere, making a pleasant disorder; and as perfume comes out of a flower, memories of singers and chandeliers rose bright from the printed names. "Norma," "Tancredi," "Don Pasquale," "La Vestale" —dim lights in the fashions of to-day—sparkled upon the exploring Gaston, conjuring the radiant halls of Europe before him. "'The Barber of Seville !' " he presently exclaimed. "And I happened to hear it in Seville."

But Seville's name brought over the padre a new rush of home thoughts. "Is not Andalusia beautiful?" he said. "Did you see it in April, when the flowers come?"

"Yes," said Gaston, among the music. "I was at Cordova then."

"Ah, Cordova !" murmured the padre.

"'Semiramide !' " cried Gaston, lighting upon that opera. "That was a week! I should like to live it over, every day and night of it!"

"Did you reach Malaga from Marseilles or Gibraltar?" said the padre, wistfully.

"From Marseilles. Down from Paris through the Rhone Valley, you know."

"Then you saw Provence! And did you go, perhaps, from Avignon to Nismes by the Pont du Gard? There is a place I have made here —a little, little place—with olive-trees. And now they have grown, and it looks something like that country, if you stand in a particular position. I will take you there to-morrow. I think you will understand what I mean."

"Another resemblance!" said the volatile and happy Gaston. "We both seem to have an eye for them. But, believe me, padre, I could never stay here planting olives. I should go back and see the original ones—and then

I'd hasten up to Paris." And, with a volume of Meyerbeer open in his hand, Gaston hummed : "'Robert, Robert, toi que j'aime.' Why, padre, I think that your library contains none of the masses and all of the operas in the world!"

"I will make you a little confession," said Padre Ignazio, "and then you shall give me a little absolution."

"With a penance," said Gaston. "You must play over some of these things to me."

"I suppose that I could not permit myself this indulgence," began the padre, pointing to his operas ; "and teach these to my choir, if the people had any worldly associations with the music. But I have reasoned that the music cannot do them harm—"

The ringing of a bell here interrupted him. "In fifteen minutes," he said, "our poor meal will be ready for you." The good padre was not quite sincere when he spoke of a poor meal. While getting the *aguardiente* for his guest he had given orders, and he knew how well such orders could be carried out. He lived alone, and generally supped simply enough, but not even the ample table at San Fernando could surpass his own on occasions. And this was for him an occasion indeed !

"Your half-breeds will think I am one of themselves," said Gaston, showing his dusty

clothes. "I am not fit to be seated with you."
He, too, was not more sincere than his host.
In his pack, which an Indian had brought from
his horse, he carried some garments of civilization. And presently, after fresh water and
not a little painstaking with brush and scarf,
there came back to the padre a young guest
whose elegance and bearing and ease of the
great world were to the exiled priest as sweet
as was his travelled conversation.

They repaired to the hall and took their seats
at the head of the long table. For the stately
Spanish centuries of custom lived at Santa
Ysabel del Mar, inviolate, feudal, remote.

They were the only persons of quality present; and between themselves and the *gente de
razon* a space intervened. Behind the padre's
chair stood an Indian to wait upon him, and
another stood behind the chair of Gaston Villeré. Each of these servants wore one single
white garment, and offered the many dishes
to the *gente fina* and refilled their glasses. At
the lower end of the table a general attendant
waited upon the *mesclados* — the half - breeds.
There was meat with spices, and roasted quail,
with various cakes and other preparations of
grain; also the black fresh olives, and grapes,
with several sorts of figs and plums, and preserved fruits, and white and red wine — the

white fifty years old. Beneath the quiet shining of candles, fresh - cut flowers leaned from vessels of old Mexican and Spanish make.

There at one end of this feast sat the wild, pastoral, gaudy company, speaking little over their food; and there at the other the pale padre, questioning his visitor about Rachel. The mere name of a street would bring memories crowding to his lips; and when his guest would tell him of a new play, he was ready with old quotations from the same author. Alfred de Vigny they had, and Victor Hugo, whom the padre disliked. Long after the *dulce*, or sweet dish, when it was the custom for the vaqueros and the rest of the retainers to rise and leave the *gente fina* to themselves, the host sat on in the empty hall, fondly telling the guest of his bygone Paris, and fondly learning of the Paris that was to-day. And thus the two lingered, exchanging their fervors, while the candles waned, and the long-haired Indians stood silent behind the chairs.

"But we must go to my piano," the host exclaimed. For at length they had come to a lusty difference of opinion. The padre, with ears critically deaf, and with smiling, unconvinced eyes, was shaking his head, while young Gaston sang "Trovatore" at him, and beat upon the table with a fork.

"Come and convert me, then," said Padre Ignazio, and he led the way. "Donizetti I have always admitted. There, at least, is refinement. If the world has taken to this Verdi, with his street-band music— But there, now! Sit down and convert me. Only don't crush my poor little Erard with Verdi's hoofs. I brought it when I came. It is behind the times too. And, oh, my dear boy, our organ is still worse. So old, so old! To get a proper one I would sacrifice even this piano of mine in a moment—only the tinkling thing is not worth a sou to anybody except its master. But there! Are you quite comfortable?" And having seen to his guest's needs, and placed spirits and cigars and an ash-tray within his reach, the padre sat himself luxuriously in his chair to hear and expose the false doctrine of "Il Trovatore."

By midnight all of the opera that Gaston could recall had been played and sung twice. The convert sat in his chair no longer, but stood singing by the piano. The potent swing and flow of tunes, the torrid, copious inspiration of the South, mastered him. "Verdi has grown," he cried. "Verdi has become a giant." And he swayed to the beat of the melodies, and waved an enthusiastic arm. He demanded every crumb. Why did not Gaston remember it all? But if the barkentine would arrive and bring the whole music, then they would have it right! And he made Gaston teach him what words he knew. "'Non ti scordar,'" he sang—"'non ti scordar di me.' That is genius. But one sees how the world moves when one is out of it. 'A nostri monti ritorneremo;' home to our mountains. Ah, yes, there is genius again." And the exile sighed and his spirit went to distant places, while Gaston continued brilliantly with the music of the final scene.

Then the host remembered his guest. "I am ashamed of my selfishness," he said. "It is already to-morrow."

"I have sat later in less good company," answered the pleasant Gaston. "And I shall sleep all the sounder for making a convert."

"You have dispensed roadside alms," said the padre, smiling. "And that should win excellent dreams."

Thus, with courtesies more elaborate than the world has time for at the present day, they bade each other good-night and parted, bearing their late candles along the quiet halls of the mission. To young Gaston in his bed easy sleep came without waiting, and no dreams at all. Outside his open window was the quiet, serene darkness, where the stars shone clear, and tranquil perfumes hung in the cloisters. And while the guest lay sleeping all night in unchanged position like a child, up and down between the oleanders went Padre Ignazio, walking until dawn.

Day showed the ocean's surface no longer glassy, but lying like a mirror breathed upon; and there between the short headlands came a sail, gray and plain against the flat water. The priest watched through his glasses, and saw the gradual sun grow strong upon the canvas of the barkentine. The message from his world was at hand, yet to-day he scarcely cared so much. Sitting in his garden yesterday he could never have imagined such a change. But his heart did not hail the barkentine as usual. Books, music, pale paper, and print—this was all that was coming to him, and some of its savor had gone; for the siren voice of life had been speaking with him face to face, and in his spirit, deep down, the love of the world was restlessly answering that call. Young Gaston showed more eagerness than the padre over this arrival of the vessel that might be bringing "Trovatore" in the nick of time. Now he would have the chance, before he took his leave, to help rehearse the new music with the choir. He would be a missionary too. A perfectly new experience.

"And you still forgive Verdi the sins of his youth?" he said to his host. "I wonder if you could forgive mine?"

"Verdi has left his behind him," retorted the padre.

"But I am only twenty-five," explained Gaston, pathetically.

"Ah, don't go away soon!" pleaded the exile. It was the plainest burst that had escaped him, and he felt instant shame.

But Gaston was too much elated with the enjoyment of each new day to understand. The shafts of another's pain might scarcely pierce the bright armor of his gayety. He mistook the priest's exclamation for anxiety about his own happy soul.

"Stay here under your care?" he said. "It would do me no good, padre. Temptation sticks closer to me than a brother!" and he gave that laugh of his which disarmed severer judges than his host. "By next week I should have introduced some sin or other into your beautiful Garden of Ignorance here. It will be much safer for your flock if I go and join the other serpents at San Francisco."

Soon after breakfast the padre had his two mules saddled, and he and his guest set forth down the hills together to the shore. And beneath the spell and confidence of pleasant, slow riding, and the loveliness of everything, the young man talked freely of himself.

"And, seriously," said he, "if I missed nothing else at Santa Ysabel, I should long to hear the birds. At home our gardens are full of them, and one smells the jasmine, and they sing and sing! When our ship from the Isthmus put into San Diego, I decided to go on by land and see California. Then, after the first days, I began to miss something. All that beauty seemed empty, in a way. And suddenly I found it was the birds. For these little scampering quail are nothing. There seems a sort of death in the air where no birds ever sing."

"You will not find any birds at San Francisco," said the padre.

"I shall find life!" exclaimed Gaston. "And my fortune at the mines, I hope. I am not a bad fellow, father. You can easily guess all the things that I do. I have never, to my knowledge, harmed any one. I did not even try to kill my adversary in an affair of honor. I gave him a mere flesh wound, and by this time he must be quite recovered. He was my friend. But as he came between me—"

Gaston stopped; and the padre, looking keenly at him, saw the violence that he had noticed in church pass like a flame over the young man's handsome face.

"There's nothing dishonorable," said Gaston, answering the priest's look.

"I have not thought so, my son."

"I did what every gentleman would do," said Gaston.

"And that is often wrong!" cried the padre. "But I'm not your confessor."

"I've nothing to confess," said Gaston, frankly. "I left New Orleans at once, and have travelled an innocent journey straight to you. And when I make my fortune I shall be in a position to return and—"

"Claim the pressed flower!" put in the padre, laughing.

"Ah, you remember how those things are!" said Gaston; and he laughed also and blushed.

"Yes," said the padre, looking at the anchored barkentine, "I remember how those things are." And for a while the vessel and its cargo and the landed men and various business and conversations occupied them. But the freight for the mission once seen to, there was not much else to hang about here for.

The barkentine was only a coaster like many others which now had begun to fill the sea a little more of late years, and presently host and guest were riding homeward. And guessing at the two men from their outsides, any one would have got them precisely wrong; for within the turbulent young figure of Gaston dwelt a spirit that could not be more at ease, while revolt was steadily smouldering beneath the schooled and placid mask of the padre.

Yet still the strangeness of his being at such a place came back as a marvel into the young man's lively mind. Twenty years in prison, he thought, and hardly aware of it! And he glanced at the silent priest. A man so evidently fond of music, of theatres, of the world, to whom pressed flowers had meant something once—and now contented to bleach upon these wastes! Not even desirous of a brief holiday, but finding an old organ and some old operas enough recreation! "It is his age, I suppose," thought Gaston. And then the notion of himself when he should be sixty occurred to him, and he spoke.

"Do you know, I do not believe," said he, "that I should ever reach such contentment as yours."

"Perhaps you will," said Padre Ignazio, in a low voice.

"Never!" declared the youth. "It comes only to the few, I am sure."

"Yes. Only to the few," murmured the padre.

"I am certain that it must be a great possession," Gaston continued; "and yet—and yet—dear me! life is a splendid thing!"

"There are several sorts of it," said the padre.

"Only one for me!" cried Gaston. "Action, men, women, things—to be there, to be known, to play a part, to sit in the front seats; to have people tell each other, 'There goes Gaston Villeré!' and to deserve one's prominence. Why, if I were Padre of Santa Ysabel del Mar for twenty years—no! for one year—do you know what I should have done? Some day it would have been too much for me. I should have left these savages to a pastor nearer their own level, and I should have ridden down this cañon upon my mule, and stepped on board the barkentine, and gone back to my proper sphere. You will understand, sir, that I am far from venturing to make any personal comment. I am only thinking what a world of difference lies between men's natures who can feel alike as we do upon so many subjects. Why, not since leaving New Orleans have I met any one with whom I could talk, except of the weather and the brute interests common to us all. That such a one as you should be here is like a dream."

"But it is not a dream," said the padre.

"And, sir—pardon me if I do say this—are you not wasted at Santa Ysabel del Mar? I have seen the priests at the other missions. They are—the sort of good men that I expected. But are you needed to save such souls as these?"

"There is no aristocracy of souls," said the padre, almost whispering now.

"But the body and the mind!" cried Gaston. "My God, are they nothing? Do you think that they are given to us for nothing but a trap? You cannot teach such a doctrine with your library there. And how about all the cultivated men and women away from whose quickening society the brightest of us grow numb? You have held out. But will it be for long? Do you not owe yourself to the saving of higher game henceforth? Are not twenty years of *mesclados* enough? No, no!" finished young Gaston, hot with his unforeseen eloquence; "I should ride down some morning and take the barkentine."

Padre Ignazio was silent for a space.

"I have not offended you?" said the young man.

"No. Anything but that. You are surprised that I should — choose — to stay here. Perhaps you may have wondered how I came to be here at all?"

208

"I had not intended any impertinent—"

"Oh no. Put such an idea out of your head, my son. You may remember that I was going to make you a confession about my operas. Let us sit down in this shade."

So they picketed the mules near the stream and sat down.

"You have seen," began Padre Ignazio, "what sort of a man I—was once. Indeed, it seems very strange to myself that you should have been here not twenty-four hours yet, and know so much of me. For there has come no one else at all"—the padre paused a moment and mastered the unsteadiness that he had felt approaching in his voice—"there has been no one else to whom I have talked so freely. In my early days I had no thought of being a priest. My parents destined me for a diplomatic career. There was plenty of money and —and all the rest of it; for by inheritance came to me the acquaintance of many people whose names you would be likely to have heard of. Cities, people of fashion, artists — the whole of it was my element and my choice; and by-and-by I married, not only where it was desirable, but where I loved. Then for the first time Death laid his staff upon my enchantment, and I understood many things that had been only words to me hitherto. Looking back, it seemed to me that I had never done anything except for myself all my days. I left the world. In due time I became a priest and lived in my own country. But my worldly experience and my secular education had given to my opinions a turn too liberal for the place where my work was laid. I was soon advised concerning this by those in authority over me. And since they could not change me and I could not change them, yet wished to work and to teach, the New World was suggested, and I volunteered to give the rest of my life to missions. It was soon found that some one was needed here, and for this little place I sailed, and to these humble people I have dedicated my service. They are pastoral creatures of the soil. Their vineyard and cattle days are apt to be like the sun and storm around them —strong alike in their evil and in their good. All their years they live as children—children with men's passions given to them like deadly weapons, unable to measure the harm their impulses may bring. Hence, even in their crimes, their hearts will generally open soon to the one great key of love, while civilization makes locks which that key cannot always fit at the first turn. And coming to know this," said Padre Ignazio, fixing his eyes steadily upon Gaston, "you will understand how great a privilege it is to help such people, and how the sense of something accomplished—under God—should bring contentment with renunciation."

"Yes," said Gaston Villeré. Then, thinking of himself, "I can understand it in a man like you."

"Do not speak of me at all!" exclaimed the padre, almost passionately. "But pray Heaven that you may find the thing yourself some day —contentment with renunciation—and never let it go."

"Amen!" said Gaston, strangely moved.

"That is the whole of my story," the priest continued, with no more of the recent stress in his voice. "And now I have talked to you about myself quite enough. But you must have my confession." He had now resumed entirely his half-playful tone. "I was just a little mistaken, you see—too self-reliant, perhaps—when I supposed, in my first missionary ardor, that I could get on without any remembrance of the world at all. I found that I could not. And so I have taught the old operas to my choir—such parts of them as are within our compass and suitable for worship. And certain of my friends still alive at home are good enough to remember this taste of mine, and to send me each year some of the new

211

music that I should never hear of otherwise.
Then we study these things also. And although
our organ is a miserable affair, Felipe manages
very cleverly to make it do. And while the
voices are singing these operas, especially the
old ones, what harm is there if sometimes the
priest is thinking of something else? So there's
my confession! And now, whether 'Trovatore' has come or not, I shall not allow you to
leave us until you have taught all you know
of it to Felipe."

The new opera, however, had duly arrived.
And as he turned its pages Padre Ignazio was
quick to seize at once upon the music that
could be taken into his church. Some of it
was ready fitted. By that afternoon Felipe
and his choir could have rendered "Ah! se l'
error t' ingombra" without slip or falter.

Those were strange rehearsals of "Il Trovatore" upon this California shore. For the padre
looked to Gaston to say when they went too
fast or too slow, and to correct their emphasis.
And since it was hot, the little Erard piano
was carried each day out into the mission
garden. There, in the cloisters among the
oleanders, in the presence of the tall yellow
hills and the blue triangle of sea, the "Mis-
erere" was slowly learned. The Mexicans and
Indians gathered, swarthy and black-haired,

around the tinkling instrument that Felipe played; and presiding over them were young Gaston and the pale padre, walking up and down the paths, beating time, or singing now one part and now another. And so it was that the wild cattle on the uplands would hear "Trovatore" hummed by a passing vaquero, while the same melody was filling the streets of the far-off world.

For three days Gaston Villeré remained at Santa Ysabel del Mar; and though not a word of the sort came from him, his host could read San Francisco and the gold-mines in his countenance. No, the young man could not have stayed here for twenty years! And the padre forbore urging his guest to extend his visit.

"But the world is small," the guest declared at parting. "Some day it will not be able to spare you any longer. And then we are sure to meet. And you shall hear from me soon, at any rate."

Again, as upon the first evening, the two exchanged a few courtesies, more graceful and particular than we, who have not time, and fight no duels, find worth a man's while at the present day. For duels are gone, which is a very good thing, and with them a certain careful politeness, which is a pity; but that is the way in the general profit and loss. So young

Gaston rode northward out of the mission, back to the world and his fortune; and the padre stood watching the dust after the rider had passed from sight. Then he went into his room with a drawn face. But appearances at least had been kept up to the end; the youth would never know of the old man's discontent.

Temptation had arrived with Gaston, but was going to make a longer stay at Santa Ysabel del Mar. Yet it was something like a week before the priest knew what guest he had in his house now. The guest was not always present—made himself scarce quite often.

Sail away on the barkentine? That was a wild notion, to be sure, although fit enough to enter the brain of such a young scapegrace. The padre shook his head and smiled affectionately when he thought of Gaston Villeré. The youth's handsome, reckless countenance would come before him, and he repeated Auber's old remark, " Is it the good Lord, or is it merely the devil, that always make me have a weakness for rascals?"

Sail away on the barkentine! Imagine taking leave of the people here — of Felipe! In what words should he tell the boy to go on industriously with his music? No, this could not be imagined. The mere parting alone would make it forever impossible that he should think of such a thing. "And then," he said to himself each new morning, when he looked out at the ocean, "I have given my life to them. One does not take back a gift."

Pictures of his departure began to shine and melt in his drifting fancy. He saw himself explaining to Felipe that now his presence was wanted elsewhere; that there would come a successor to take care of Santa Ysabel—a younger man, more useful, and able to visit sick people at a distance. "For I am old now. I should not be long here in any case." He stopped and pressed his hands together ; he had caught his temptation in the very act. Now he sat staring at his temptation's face, close to him, while there in the triangle two ships went sailing by.

One morning Felipe told him that the barkentine was here on its return voyage south. "Indeed?" said the padre, coldly. "The things are ready to go, I think." For the vessel called for mail and certain boxes that the mission sent away. Felipe left the room, in wonder at the padre's manner. But the priest was laughing alone inside to see how little it was to him where the barkentine was, or whether it should be coming or going. But in the afternoon, at his piano, he found himself saying, "Other ships call here, at any rate." And then

215

for the first time he prayed to be delivered from his thoughts. Yet presently he left his seat and looked out of the window for a sight of the barkentine; but it was gone.

The season of the wine-making passed, and the putting up of all the fruits that the mission fields grew. Lotions and medicines were distilled from the garden herbs. Perfume was manufactured from the petals of the flowers and certain spices, and presents of it despatched to San Fernando and Ventura, and to friends at other places; for the padre had a special receipt. As the time ran on, two or three visitors passed a night with him; and presently there was a word at various missions that Padre Ignazio had begun to show his years. At Santa Ysabel del Mar they whispered, "The padre is getting sick." Yet he rode a great deal over the hills by himself, and down the cañon very often, stopping where he had sat with Gaston, to sit alone and look up and down, now at the hills above, and now at the ocean below. Among his parishioners he had certain troubles to soothe, certain wounds to heal; a home from which he was able to drive jealousy; a girl whom he bade her lover set right. But all said, "The padre is sick." And Felipe told them that the music seemed nothing to him any more; he never asked for his

Dixit Dominus nowadays. Then for a short time he was really in bed, feverish with the two voices that spoke to him without ceasing. "You have given your life," said one voice. "And therefore," said the other, "have earned the right to go home and die." "You are winning better rewards in the service of God," said the first voice. "God can be served in other places than this," answered the second. As he lay listening he saw Seville again, and the trees of Aranhal, where he had been born. The wind was blowing through them, and in their branches he could hear the nightingales. "Empty! Empty!" he said, aloud. "He was right about the birds. Death does live in the air where they never sing." And he lay for two days and nights hearing the wind and the nightingales in the trees of Aranhal. But Felipe, watching, heard only the padre crying through the hours: "Empty! Empty!"

Then the wind in the trees died down, and the padre could get out of bed, and soon could be in the garden. But the voices within him still talked all the while as he sat watching the sails when they passed between the headlands. Their words, falling forever the same way, beat his spirit sore, like bruised flesh. If he could only change what they said, he could rest.

"Has the padre any mail for Santa Bar-

217

bara ?" said Felipe. "The ship bound southward should be here to-morrow."

"I will attend to it," said the priest, not
moving. And Felipe stole away.

At Felipe's words the voices had stopped, as
a clock done striking. Silence, strained like
expectation, filled the padre's soul. But in
place of the voices came old sights of home
again, the waving trees at Aranhal; then it
would be Rachel for a moment, declaiming
tragedy while a houseful of faces that he knew
by name watched her; and through all the
panorama rang the pleasant laugh of Gaston.
For a while in the evening the padre sat
at his Erard playing "Trovatore." Later,
in his sleepless bed he lay, saying now and
then: "To die at home! Surely I may be
granted at least this." And he listened for the
inner voices. But they were not speaking any
more, and the black hole of silence grew more
dreadful to him than their arguments. Then
the dawn came in at his window, and he lay
watching its gray grow warm into color, until
suddenly he sprang from his bed and looked at
the sea. The south-bound ship was coming.
People were on board who in a few weeks
would be sailing the Atlantic, while he would
stand here looking out of the same window.
"Merciful God!" he cried, sinking on his

knees. "Heavenly Father, Thou seest this evil in my heart. Thou knowest that my weak hand cannot pluck it out. My strength is breaking, and still Thou makest my burden heavier than I can bear." He stopped, breathless and trembling. The same visions were flitting across his closed eyes ; the same silence gaped like a dry crater in his soul. "There is no help in earth or heaven," he said, very quietly ; and he dressed himself.

It was so early still that none but a few of the Indians were stirring, and one of them saddled the padre's mule. Felipe was not yet awake, and for a moment it came in the priest's mind to open the boy's door softly, look at him once more, and come away. But this he did not do, nor even take a farewell glance at the church and organ. He bade nothing farewell, but, turning his back upon his room and his garden, rode down the cañon.

The vessel lay at anchor, and some one had landed from her and was talking with other men on the shore. Seeing the priest slowly coming, this stranger approached to meet him.

"You are connected with the mission here?" he inquired.

"I—am."

"Perhaps it is with you that Gaston Villeré stopped?"

"The young man from New Orleans? Yes. I am Padre Ignazio."

"Then you will save me a journey. I promised him to deliver these into your own hands."

The stranger gave them to him.

"A bag of gold-dust," he explained, "and a letter. I wrote it from his dictation while he was dying. He lived scarcely an hour afterwards."

The stranger bowed his head at the stricken cry which his news elicited from the priest, who, after a few moments' vain effort to speak, opened the letter and read:

"MY DEAR FRIEND,—It is through no man's fault but mine that I have come to this. I have had plenty of luck, and lately have been counting the days until I should return home. But last night heavy news from New Orleans reached me, and I tore the pressed flower to pieces. Under the first smart and humiliation of broken faith I was rendered desperate, and picked a needless quarrel. Thank God, it is I who have the punishment. My dear friend, as I lie here, leaving a world that no man ever loved more, I have come to understand you. For you and your mission have been much in my thoughts. It is strange how good can be done, not at the time when it is intended, but afterwards; and you have done this good to me. I say over your words, 'contentment with renunciation,' and believe that at this last hour I have gained something like what you would wish me to feel. For I do not think that I desire it otherwise now. My life would never have been of service, I am afraid. You are the last person in this world who has spoken serious words to me, and I want you to know that now at length I value the peace of Santa Ysabel as I could never have done but for seeing your wisdom and goodness. You spoke of a new organ for your church. Take the gold-dust that will reach you with this, and do what you will with it. Let me at least in dying have helped some one. And since there is no aristocracy in souls—you said that to me; do you remember?—perhaps you will say a mass for this departing soul of mine. I only wish, since my body must go underground in a strange country, that it might have been at Santa Ysabel del Mar, where your feet would often pass."

"'At Santa Ysabel del Mar, where your feet would often pass.'" The priest repeated this final sentence aloud, without being aware of it.

"Those are the last words he ever spoke," said the stranger, "except bidding good-bye to me."

"You knew him well, then?"

"No; not until after he was hurt. I'm the man he quarrelled with."

The priest looked at the ship that would sail onward this afternoon. Then a smile of great beauty passed over his face, and he addressed

221

the stranger. "I thank you," said he. "You will never know what you have done for me."

"It is nothing," answered the stranger, awkwardly. "He told me you set great store on a new organ."

Padre Ignazio turned away from the ship and rode back through the gorge. When he reached the shady place where once he had sat with Gaston Villeré, he dismounted and again sat there, alone by the stream, for many hours. Long rides and outings had been lately so much his custom, that no one thought twice of his absence; and when he returned to the mission in the afternoon, the Indian took his mule, and he went to his seat in the garden. But it was with another look that he watched the sea; and presently the sail moved across the blue triangle, and soon it had rounded the headland. Gaston's first coming was in the padre's mind; and as the vespers bell began to ring in the cloistered silence, a fragment of Auber's plaintive tune passed like a sigh across his memory:

But for the repose of Gaston's soul they sang all that he had taught them of "Il Trovatore."

Thus it happened that Padre Ignazio never went home, but remained cheerful master of the desires to do so that sometimes visited him, until the day came when he was called altogether away from this world, and "passed beyond these voices, where is peace."

Napoleon Shave-Tail

AUGUSTUS ALBUMBLATT, young and new and sleek with the latest book-knowledge of war, reported to his first troop commander at Fort Brown. The ladies had watched for him, because he would increase the number of men, the officers because he would lessen the number of duties; and he joined at a crisis favorable to becoming speedily known by them all. Upon that same day had household servants become an extinct race. The last one, the commanding officer's cook, had told the commanding officer's wife that she was used to living where she could see the cars. She added that there was no society here "fit for man or baste at all." This opinion was formed on the preceding afternoon when Casey, a sergeant of roguish attractions in G troop, had told her that he was not a marrying man. Three hours later she wedded a gambler, and this morning at six they had taken the stage for Green River, two hundred miles

227

south, the nearest point where the bride could see the cars.

"Frank," said the commanding officer's wife, "send over to H troop for York."

"Catherine," he answered, "my dear, our statesmen at Washington say it's wicked to hire the free American soldier to cook for you. It's too menial for his manhood."

"Frank, stuff!"

"Hush, my love. Therefore York must be spared the insult of twenty more dollars a month, our statesmen must be re-elected, and you and I, Catherine, being cookless, must join the general mess."

Thus did all separate housekeeping end, and the garrison began unitedly to eat three times a day what a Chinaman set before them, when the long-expected Albumblatt stepped into their midst, just in time for supper.

This youth was spic-and-span from the Military Academy, with a top-dressing of three months' thoughtful travel in Germany. "I was deeply impressed with the modernity of their scientific attitude," he pleasantly remarked to the commanding officer. For Captain Duane, silent usually, talked at this first meal to make the boy welcome in this forlorn two-company post.

"We're cut off from all that sort of thing

here," said he. "I've not been east of the Missouri since '69. But we've got the railroad across, and we've killed some Indians, and we've had some fun, and we're glad we're alive —eh, Mrs. Starr?"

"I should think so," said the lady.

"Especially now we've got a bachelor at the post!" said Mrs. Bainbridge. "That has been the one drawback, Mr. Albumblatt."

"I thank you for the compliment," said Augustus, bending solemnly from his hips; and Mrs. Starr looked at him and then at Mrs. Bainbridge.

"We're not over-gay, I fear," the Captain continued; "but the flat's full of antelope, and there's good shooting up both cañons."

"Have you followed the recent target experiments at Metz?" inquired the traveller. "I refer to the flattened trajectory and the obus controversy."

"We have not heard the reports," answered the commandant, with becoming gravity. "But we own a mountain howitzer."

"The modernity of German ordnance—" began Augustus.

"Do you dance, Mr. Albumblatt?" asked Mrs. Starr.

"For we'll have a hop and all be your part-ners," Mrs. Bainbridge exclaimed.

"I will be pleased to accommodate you, ladies."

"It's anything for variety's sake with us, you see," said Mrs. Starr, smoothly smiling; and once again Augustus bent blandly from his hips.

But the commanding officer wished leniency. "You see us all," he hastened to say. "Commissioned officers and dancing-men. Pretty shabby—"

"Oh, Captain!" said a lady.

"And pretty old."

"*Captain!*" said another lady.

"But alive and kicking. Captain Starr, Mr. Bainbridge, the Doctor and me. We are seven."

Augustus looked accurately about him. "Do I understand seven, Captain?"

"We are seven," the senior officer repeated.

Again Mr. Albumblatt counted heads. "I imagine you include the ladies, Captain? Ha! ha!"

"Seven commissioned males, sir. Our Major is on sick-leave, and two of our Lieutenants are related to the President's wife. She can't bear them to be exposed. None of us in the church-yard lie—but we are seven."

"Ha! ha, Captain! That's an elegant double-entendre on Wordsworth's poem and the War Department. Only, if I may correct your ad-

230

dition—ha! ha!—our total, including myself, is eight." And Augustus grew as hilarious as a wooden nutmeg.

The commanding officer rolled an intimate eye at his wife.

The lady was sitting big with rage, but her words were cordial still: "Indeed, Mr. Albumblatt, the way officers who have influence in Washington shirk duty here and get details East is something I can't laugh about. At one time the Captain was his own adjutant and quartermaster. There are more officers at this table to-night than I've seen in three years. So we are doubly glad to welcome you at Fort Brown."

"I am fortunate to be on duty where my services are so required, though I could object to calling it Fort Brown." And Augustus exhaled a new smile.

"Prefer Smith?" said Captain Starr.

"You misunderstand me. When we say *Fort* Brown. *Fort* Russell, *Fort* Et Cetera, we are inexact. They are not fortified."

"Cantonment Et Cetera would be a trifle lengthy, wouldn't it?" put in the Doctor, his endurance on the wane.

"Perhaps; but technically descriptive of our Western posts. The Germans criticise these military laxities."

231

Captain Duane now ceased talking, but urbanely listened ; and from time to time his eye would scan Augustus, and then a certain sublimated laugh, to his wife well known, would seize him for a single voiceless spasm, and pass. The experienced Albumblatt meanwhile continued, "By-the-way, Doctor, you know the Charité, of course?"

Doctor Guild had visited that great hospital, but being now a goaded man he stuck his nose in his plate, and said, unwisely : "Sharrity? What's that?" For then Augustus told him what and where it was, and that Krankenhaus is German for hospital, and that he had been deeply impressed with the modernity of the ventilation. "Thirty-five cubic metres to a bed in new wards," he stated. "How many do you allow, Doctor?"

"None," answered the surgeon.

"Do I understand none, Doctor?"

"You do, sir. My patients breathe in cubic feet, and swallow their doses in grains, and have their inflation measured in inches."

"Now there again!" exclaimed Augustus, cheerily. "More antiquity to be swept away! And people say we young officers have no work cut out for us!"

"Patients don't die then under the metric system?" said the Doctor.

"No wonder Europe's overcrowded," said Starr.

But the student's mind inhabited heights above such trifling. "Death," he said, "occurs in ratios not differentiated from our statistics." And he told them much more while they looked at him over their plates. He managed to say 'modernity' and 'differentiate' again, for he came from our middle West, where they encounter education too suddenly, and it would take three generations of him to speak clean English. But with all his polysyllabic wallowing, he showed himself keen-minded, pat with authorities, a spruce young graduate among these dingy Rocky Mountain campaigners. They had fought and thirsted and frozen; the books that he knew were not written when they went to school; and so far as war is to be mastered on paper, his equipment was full and polished while theirs was meagre and rusty.

And yet, if you know things that other and older men do not, it is as well not to mention them too hastily. These soldiers wished that they could have been taught what he knew; but they watched young Augustus unfolding himself with a gaze that might have seemed chill to a less highly abstract thinker. He, however, rose from the table pleasantly edified by himself, and hopeful for them. And as he left them, "Good-night, ladies and gentlemen," he said ; "we shall meet again."

"Oh yes," said the Doctor. "Again and again."

"He's given me indigestion," said Bainbridge.

"Take some metric system," said Starr.

"And lie flat on your trajectory," said the Doctor.

"I hate hair parted in the middle for a man," said Mrs. Guild.

"And his superior eye-glasses," said Mrs. Bainbridge.

"His staring conceited teeth," hissed Mrs. Starr.

"I don't like children slopping their knowledge all over me," said the Doctor's wife.

"He's well brushed, though," said Mrs. Duane, seeking the bright side. "He'll wipe his feet on the mat when he comes to call."

"I'd rather have mud on my carpet than that bandbox in any of my chairs," said Mrs. Starr.

"He's no fool," mused the Doctor. "But, kingdom come, what an ass !"

"Well, gentlemen," said the commanding officer (and they perceived a flavor of the official in his tone), "Mr. Albumblatt is just twenty-one. I don't know about you; but I'll never have that excuse again."

"Very well, Captain, we'll be good," said Mrs. Bainbridge.

"And gr-r-ateful," said Mrs. Starr, rolling her r piously. "I prophecy he'll entertain us."

The Captain's demeanor remained slightly official; but walking home, his Catherine by his side in the dark was twice aware of that laugh of his, twinkling in the recesses of his opinions. And later, going to bed, a little joke took him so unready that it got out before he could suppress it. "My love," said he, "my Second Lieutenant is grievously mislaid in the cavalry. Providence designed him for the artillery."

It was wifely but not right in Catherine to repeat this strict confidence in strictest confidence to her neighbor, Mrs. Bainbridge, over the fence next morning before breakfast. At breakfast Mrs. Bainbridge spoke of artillery reinforcing the post, and her husband giggled girlishly and looked at the puzzled Duane; and at dinner Mrs. Starr asked Albumblatt, would not artillery strengthen the garrison?

"Even a light battery," pronounced Augustus, promptly, "would be absurd and useless."

Whereupon the mess rattled knives, sneezed, and became variously disturbed. So they called him Albumbattery, and then Blattery, which is more condensed; and Captain Duane's official tone availed him nothing in this matter. But he made no more little military jokes; he disliked garrison personalities. Civilized by birth and ripe from weather-beaten years of men and observing, he looked his Second Lieutenant over, and remembered to have seen worse than this. He had no quarrel with the metric system (truly the most sensible), and thinking to leaven it with a little rule of thumb, he made Augustus his acting quartermaster. But he presently indulged his wife with the soldier-cook she wanted at home, so they no longer had to eat their meals in Albumblatt's society; and Mrs. Starr said that this showed her husband dreaded his quartermaster worse than the Secretary of War.

Alas for the Quartermaster's sergeant, Johannes Schmoll, that routined and clock-work German! He found Augustus so much more German than he had ever been himself, that he went speechless for three days. Upon his lists, his red ink, and his ciphering, Augustus swooped like a bird of prey, and all his fond red-tape devices were shredded to the winds. Augustus set going new quadratic ones of his own, with an index and cross-references. It was then that Schmoll recovered his speech and walked alone, saying, "Mein Gott!" And often thereafter, wandering among the piled stores and apparel, he would fling both arms heavenward and repeat the exclamation. He had rated himself the unique human soul at Fort Brown able to count and arrange underclothing. Augustus rejected his laborious tally, and together they vigiled after hours, verifying socks and drawers. Next, Augustus found more horseshoes than his papers called for.

"That man gif me der stomach pain efry day," wailed Schmoll to Sergeant Casey. "I tell him, 'Lieutenant, dose horseshoes is expendable. We don't acgount for efry shoe like they was men's shoes, und oder dings dot is issued.' 'I prefer to dake them oop!' says Baby Bismarck. Und he smile mit his two beaver teeth."

"Baby Bismarck!" cried, joyfully, the rosy-faced Casey. "Yo-hanny, take a drink."

"Und so," continued the outraged Schmoll, "he haf a Board of Soorvey on dree-pound horseshoes, und I haf der stomach pain."

It was buckles the next month. The allowance exceeded the expenditure, Augustus's arithmetic came out wrong, and another board sat on buckles.

"Yo-hanny, you're lookin' jaded under Colonel Safetypin." said Casey. "Have something."

"Safetypin is my treat," said Schmoll; "und very apt."

But Augustus found leisure to pervade the post with his modernity. He set himself military problems, and solved them; he wrote an essay on "The Contact Squadron"; he corrected Bainbridge for saying "throw back the left flank" instead of "refuse the left flank"; he had reading-room ideas, canteen ideas, ideas for the Indians and the Agency, and recruit-drill ideas, which he presented to Sergeant Casey. Casey gave him, in exchange, the name of Napoleon Shave-Tail, and had his whiskey again paid for by the sympathetic Schmoll.

"But bless his educated heart," said Casey, "he don't learn me nothing that 'll soil my innercence!"

Thus did the sunny-humored Sergeant take it, but not thus the mess. Had Augustus seen himself as they saw him, could he have heard Mrs. Starr— But he did not; the youth was impervious, and to remove his complacency would require (so Mrs. Starr said) an operation, probably fatal. The commanding officer held always aloof from gibing, yet often when Augustus passed him his gray eye would dwell upon the Lieutenant's back, and his voiceless laugh would possess him. That is the picture I retain of these days—the unending golden

sun, the wide, gentle-colored plain, the splen'
did mountains, the Indians ambling through
the flat, clear distance; and here, close along
the parade-ground, eye-glassed Augustus, neat-
ly hastening, with the Captain on his porch,
asleep you might suppose.

One early morning the agent, with two Indian chiefs, waited on the commanding officer,
and after their departure his wife found him
breakfasting in solitary mirth.

"Without me," she chided, sitting down.
"And I know you've had some good news."

"The best, my love. Providence has been
tempted at last. The wholesome irony of life
is about to function."

"Frank, don't tease so! And where are you
rushing now before the cakes?"

"To set our Augustus a little military problem, dearest. Plain living for to-day, and high
thinking be jolly well—"

"Frank, you're going to swear, and I *must*
know!"

But Frank had sworn and hurried out to the
right to the Adjutant's office, while his Catherine flew to the left to the fence.

"Ella!" she cried. "Oh, Ella!"

Mrs. Bainbridge, instantly on the other side
of the fence, brought scanty light. A telegram
had come, she knew, from the Crow Agency

in Montana. Her husband had admitted this three nights ago; and Captain Duane (she knew) had given him some orders about something; and could it be the Crows? "Ella, I don't know," said Catherine. "Frank talked all about Providence in his incurable way, and it may be anything." So the two ladies wondered together over the fence, until Mrs. Duane, seeing the Captain return, ran to him and asked, were the Crows on the war-path? Then her Frank told her yes, and that he had detailed Albumblatt to vanquish them and escort them to Carlisle School to learn German and Beethoven's sonatas.

"Stuff, stuff, stuff! Why, there he *does* go!" cried the unsettled Catherine. "It's something at the Agency!" But Captain Duane was gone into the house for a cigar.

Albumblatt, with Sergeant Casey and a detail of six men, was in truth hastening over that broad mile which opens between Fort Brown and the Agency. On either side of them the level plain stretched, gray with its sage, buff with intervening grass, hay-cocked with the smoky, mellow-stained, meerschaum-like canvas tepees of the Indians, quiet as a painting; far eastward lay long, low, rose-red hills, half dissolved in the trembling mystery of sun and distance; and westward, close at

240

hand and high, shone the great pale-blue serene mountains through the vaster serenity of the air. The sounding hoofs of the troops brought the Indians out of their tepees to see. When Albumblatt reached the Agency, there waited the agent and his two chiefs, who pointed to one lodge standing apart some three hundred yards, and said, "He is there." So then Augustus beheld his problem, the military duty fallen to him from Providence and Captain Duane.

It seems elementary for him who has written of "The Contact Squadron." It was to arrest one Indian. This man, Ute Jack, had done a murder among the Crows, and fled south for shelter. The telegram heralded him, but with boundless miles for hiding he had stolen in under the cover of night. No welcome met him. These Fort Brown Indians were not his friends at any time, and less so now, when he arrived wild drunk among their families. Hounded out, he sought this empty lodge, and here he was, at bay, his hand against every man's, counting his own life worthless except for destroying others before he must himself die.

"Is he armed?" Albumblatt inquired, and was told yes.

Augustus considered the peaked cone tent.

241

The opening was on this side, but a canvas drop closed it. Not much of a problem—one man inside a sack with eight outside to catch him! But the books gave no rule for this combination, and Augustus had met with nothing of the sort in Germany. He considered at some length. Smoke began to rise through the meeting poles of the tepee, leisurely and natural, and one of the chiefs said:

"Maybe Ute Jack cooking. He hungry."

"This is not a laughing matter," said Augustus to the by-standers, who were swiftly gathering. "Tell him that I command him to surrender," he added to the agent, who shouted this forthwith; and silence followed.

"Tell him I say he must come out at once," said Augustus then; and received further silence.

"He eat now," observed the chief. "Can't talk much."

"Sergeant Casey," bellowed Albumblatt, "go over there and take him out!"

"The Lootenant understands," said Casey, slowly, "that Ute Jack has got the drop on us, and there ain't no getting any drop on him."

"Sergeant, you will execute your orders without further comment."

At this amazing step the silence fell cold indeed; but Augustus was in command.

"Shall I take any men along, sir?" said Casey in his soldier's machine voice.

"Er—yes. Er—no. Er—do as you please."

The six troopers stepped forward to go, for they loved Casey; but he ordered them sharply to fall back. Then, looking in their eyes, he whispered, "Good-bye, boys, if it's to be that way," and walked to the lodge, lifted the flap, and fell, shot instantly dead through the heart. "Two bullets into him," muttered a trooper, heavily breathing as the sounds rang. "He's down," another spoke to himself with fixed eyes; and a sigh they did not know of passed among them. The two chiefs looked at Augustus and grunted short talk together; and one, with a sweeping lift of his hand out towards the tepee and the dead man by it, said, "Maybe Ute Jack only got three — four — cartridges — so!" (his fingers counted it). "After he kill three—four —men, you get him pretty good." The Indian took the white man's death thus; but the white men could not yet be even saturnine.

"This will require reinforcement," said Augustus to the audience. "The place must be attacked by a front and flank movement. It must be knocked down. I tell you I must have it knocked down. How are you to see where he is, I'd like to know, if it's not knocked down?" Augustus's voice was getting high.

"I want the howitzer," he screeched generally.

A soldier saluted, and Augustus chattered at him.

"The howitzer, the mountain howitzer, I tell you. Don't you hear me? To knock the cursed thing he's in down. Go to Captain Duane and give him my compliments, and—no, I'll go myself. Where's my horse? My horse, I tell you! It's got to be knocked down."

"If you please, Lieutenant," said the trooper, "may we have the Red Cross ambulance?"

"Red Cross? What's that for? What's that?"

"Sergeant Casey, sir. He's a-lyin' there."

"Ambulance? Certainly. The howitzer—perhaps.they're only flesh wounds. I hope they are only flesh wounds. I must have more men —you'll come with me."

From his porch Duane viewed both Augustus approach and the man stop at the hospital, and having expected a bungle, sat to hear; but at Albumblatt's mottled face he stood up quickly and said, "What's the matter?" And hearing, burst out: "Casey! Why, he was worth fifty of— Go on, Mr. Albumblatt. What next did you achieve, sir?" And as the tale was told he cooled, bitter, but official.

" Reinforcements is it, Mr. Albumblatt?"

"The howitzer, Captain."

"Good.   And G troop?"

"For my double flank movement I—"

"Perhaps you'd like H troop as reserve?"

"Not reserve, Captain. I should establish—"

"This is your duty, Mr. Albumblatt. Perform it as you can, with what force you need."

"Thank you, sir. It is not exactly a battle, but with a, so-to-speak, intrenched—"

"Take your troops and go, sir, and report to me when you have arrested your man."

Then Duane went to the hospital, and out with the ambulance, hoping that the soldier might not be dead. But the wholesome irony of life reckons beyond our calculations; and the unreproachful, sunny face of his Sergeant evoked in Duane's memory many marches through long heat and cold, back in the rough, good times.

"Hit twice, I thought they told me," said he; and the steward surmised that one had missed.

"Perhaps," mused Duane. "And perhaps it went as intended, too. What's all that fuss?"

He turned sharply, having lost Augustus among his sadder thoughts; and here were the operations going briskly. Powder - smoke in three directions at once! Here were pickets far out-lying, and a double line of skirmishers deployed in extended order, and a mounted reserve, and men standing to horse — a command of near a hundred, a pudding of pompous, incompetent, callow bosh, with Augustus by his howitzer, scientifically raising and lowering it to bear on the lone white tepee that shone in the plain. Four races were assembled to look on — the mess Chinaman, two black laundresses, all the whites in the place (on horse and foot, some with their hats left behind), and several hundred Indians in blankets. Duane had a thought to go away and leave this galling farce under the eye of Starr, for the officers were at hand also. But his second thought bade him remain ; and looking at Augustus and the howitzer, his laugh would have returned to him ; but his heart was sore for Casey.

It was an hour of strategy and cannonade, a humiliating hour, which Fort Brown tells of to this day ; and the tepee lived through it all. For it stood upon fifteen slender poles, not speedily to be chopped down by shooting lead from afar. When low bullets drilled the canvas, the chief suggested to Augustus that Ute Jack had climbed up; and when the bullets flew high, then Ute Jack was doubtless in a hole. Nor did Augustus contrive to drop a shell from the howitzer upon Ute Jack and ex-

246

plode him—a shrewd and deadly conception; the shells went beyond, except one, that ripped through the canvas, somewhat near the ground; and Augustus, dripping, turned at length, and saying, "It won't go down," stood vacantly wiping his white face. Then the two chiefs got his leave to stretch a rope between their horses and ride hard against the tepee. It was military neither in essence nor to see, but it prevailed. The tepee sank, a huge umbrella wreck along the earth, and there lay Ute Jack across the fire's slight hollow, his knee-cap gone with the howitzer shell. But no blood had flown from that; blood will not run, you know, when a man has been dead some time. One single other shot had struck him — one through his own heart. It had singed the flesh.

"You see, Mr. Albumblatt," said Duane, in the whole crowd's hearing, "he killed himself directly after killing Casey. A very rare act for an Indian, as you are doubtless aware. But if your manœuvres with his corpse have taught you anything you did not know before, we shall all be gainers."

"Captain," said Mrs. Starr, on a later day, "you and Ute Jack have ended our fun. Since the Court of Inquiry let Mr. Albumblatt off, he has not said Germany once — and that's three months to-morrow."